Our Daily Bread

BIBLE

WORD SEARCH
& ACTIVITY BOOK

VOL. 3

Our Daily Bread
Publishing.

Our Daily Bread Bible Word Search & Activity Book, Vol. 3
© 2024 by Our Daily Bread Publishing

Requests for permission to quote from this book should be directed to: Permissions Department, Our Daily Bread Publishing, PO Box 3566, Grand Rapids, MI 49501, or contact us by email at permissions@odb.org.

Scripture quotations, unless otherwise indicated, are taken from the Holy Bible, New International Version®, NIV®. Copyright © 1973, 1978, 1984, 2011 by Biblica Inc.™ Used by permission of Zondervan. All rights reserved worldwide. www.zondervan.com.

Scripture quotations marked ESV are taken from the ESV® Bible (The Holy Bible, English Standard Version®), copyright © 2001 by Crossway, a publishing ministry of Good News Publishers. Used by permission. All rights reserved.

Scripture quotations marked KJV are taken from the Authorized Version, or King James Version, of the Bible.

Scripture quotations marked NKJV are taken from the New King James Version®. Copyright © 1982 by Thomas Nelson. Used by permission. All rights reserved.

Interior design by Michael J. Williams

ISBN: 978-1-64070-302-5

Printed in the United States of America
24 25 26 27 28 29 30 31 / 8 7 6 5 4 3 2 1

BOOKS OF THE BIBLE: OLD TESTAMENT

*Number the 39 books of the
Old Testament in the correct order.*

____ 1 Chronicles

____ 1 Kings

____ 1 Samuel

____ 2 Chronicles

____ 2 Kings

____ 2 Samuel

____ Amos

____ Daniel

____ Deuteronomy

____ Ecclesiastes

____ Esther

____ Exodus

____ Ezekiel

____ Ezra

____ Genesis

____ Habakkuk

____ Haggai

____ Hosea

____ Isaiah

____ Jeremiah

____ Job

____ Joel

____ Jonah

____ Joshua

____ Judges

____ Lamentations

____ Leviticus

____ Malachi

____ Micah

____ Nahum

____ Nehemiah

____ Numbers

____ Obadiah

____ Proverbs

____ Psalms

____ Ruth

____ Song of Songs

____ Zechariah

____ Zephaniah

BOOKS OF THE BIBLE: NEW TESTAMENT

*Number the 27 books of the
New Testament in the correct order.*

_____ 1 Corinthians

_____ 1 John

_____ 1 Peter

_____ 1 Thessalonians

_____ 1 Timothy

_____ 2 Corinthians

_____ 2 John

_____ 2 Peter

_____ 2 Thessalonians

_____ 2 Timothy

_____ 3 John

_____ Acts

_____ Colossians

_____ Ephesians

_____ Galatians

_____ Hebrews

_____ James

_____ John

_____ Jude

_____ Luke

_____ Mark

_____ Matthew

_____ Philemon

_____ Philippians

_____ Revelation

_____ Romans

_____ Titus

Answer key on page 110.

JONAH AND THE HUGE FISH:
WORD SEARCH

*Words may be horizontal, vertical, or diagonal,
forward or backward, and may overlap.*

```
G R F Q D M D T R N Y Q J D S S
W V N L E E A I O T L X O E U E
W M O I T R Y I G R L U N M O A
G R O I S O S A F R E W A I U C
D Z M H T S G I R B B U H A T Z
M O I K A S G G U P Q V S L S V
V S Z P O V E R B O A R D C E X
H F M Q Z A S L X E G J J O P G
Z O D E S T R U C T I O N R M E
C W O R M A S C E A R T Q P E V
Q V S S M O I H Q X Q M G R T H
Y Y N F O N P L E A Z J V F Y G
K S O Y I O J R O M Y P O W C R
R Y G I R S A R Q R Z G L B K W
A F S P V R H A Z E S B E O X Y
H E V E N I N S A C K C L O T H
```

BELLY	NINEVEH	SAILORS
COMPASSION	OVERBOARD	SEA
DESTRUCTION	PRAYED	TARSHISH
FISH	PROCLAIMED	TEMPESTUOUS
JONAH	PROPHET	VOMITED
LORD	SACKCLOTH	WORM

*You can read this entire story in the
Old Testament book of Jonah.*

———— *Answer key on page 111.* ————

THE FRUIT OF THE SPIRIT IS . . . LOVE:
FILL IN THE BLANK

Complete the following verses about love.
Each blank holds a single word.

1. "If I speak in the tongues of men or of
   _____, but do not have love, I am only a
   resounding _____ or a clanging cymbal. If I
   have the gift of prophecy and can fathom all mysteries
   and all _____, and if I have a
   _____ that can move mountains, but do not
   have love, I am nothing. If I give all I possess to the
   _____ and give over my body to hardship
   that I may boast, but do not have _____,
   I gain nothing." (1 Corinthians 13:1–3)

2. "Hatred stirs up _____, but love covers
   over all _____." (Proverbs 10:12)

3. "Love must be _____. Hate what is evil;
   cling to what is _____." (Romans 12:9)

4. "Love does not delight in evil but rejoices with the
   _____. It always protects, always
   _____, always hopes, always perseveres."
   (1 Corinthians 13:6–7)

5. "Be completely _____ and gentle; be
   _____, bearing with one another in love."
   (Ephesians 4:2)

6. "These three remain: _____,
   _____ and love. But the greatest of these is
   _____." (1 Corinthians 13:13)

BIBLE VILLAINS: WORD SEARCH

Words may be horizontal, vertical, or diagonal, forward or backward, and may overlap.

```
J U R U H F B H X P L A M P G B
U W J Y Q Q A M X H H B X B Z Q
D A B I M E L E K H T A R S S N
A H T M I O A D K Y E A R E M V
S I D H F F A H E R O D I A S T
F T I G A J M M T D Z G G L O F
C J K N Y L Q J O M R P Z R O H
N K N A V H I R O L F C L C P G
A E I M D L E A Z T A H X A H Y
Z V R A O H J G H I N Y V W A T
D O C H Q V L E N N Z Q W S R J
T N E P R E S C Z K R A U S I E
N E B U C H A D N E Z Z A R S E
H A L I L E D H T Q B T V J E O
Y F I D W Z U A T B A E S L E T
J Q S E K E G N Q N I I L C S K
```

ABIMELEK	HERODIAS
ATHALIAH	JEZEBEL
BALAAM	JUDAS
CAIN	NEBUCHADNEZZAR
DELILAH	PHARAOH
GOLIATH	PHARISEES
HAMAN	SATAN
HEROD	SERPENT

"'There is no peace,' says the LORD, 'for the wicked.'" —Isaiah 48:22

Answer key on page 112.

RUN, RUN, RUN: CROSSWORD

"Let us run with perseverance the race marked out for us." —Hebrews 12:1

Across

2. Prophet who fled to the desert when Jezebel vowed to kill him. (1 Kings 19:3–4)

4. Disciple who ran to inspect Jesus's empty tomb. (Luke 24:12)

5. Elisha's servant who chased Naaman to request silver. (2 Kings 5:21)

7. He ran ahead and climbed a tree to see Jesus. (Luke 19:2–4)

8. Leader who fled after murdering an Egyptian. (Exodus 2:15)

9. Potiphar's wife propositioned this servant who then ran. (Genesis 39:7)

11. King Saul's attempt on this musician's life caused him to flee. (1 Samuel 19:10)

Down

1. Woman who ran to tell the disciples of Jesus's resurrection. (Luke 24:10)

3. People chased through the Red Sea by Pharaoh's army. (Exodus 14:22)

4. Believers should run their faith race in a way that wins this. (1 Corinthians 9:24)

6. Believers can run with perseverance because they are surrounded by these. (Hebrews 12:1)

9. Prophet to Nineveh who instead sailed for Spain. (Jonah 1:3)

10. Demon-filled animals that careened off a cliff and drowned. (Matthew 8:32)

JOHN 3:16–17: WORD SEARCH

Find the below bolded words in the puzzle.
Words may be horizontal, vertical, or diagonal,
forward or backward, and may overlap.

```
L  U  L  C  W  H  G  B  O  K  D  X  I  J  L
O  A  Y  S  I  O  E  C  J  D  R  E  O  L  O
E  S  N  B  P  L  R  Q  B  D  R  D  V  B  Z
X  A  Q  R  I  Y  J  L  D  R  H  U  S  O  Q
L  V  M  E  E  D  O  G  D  O  N  L  Y  O  L
L  E  V  R  S  T  M  S  P  W  X  F  B  K  N
D  E  L  W  K  C  E  K  W  H  B  J  Z  Q  E
S  E  Q  H  M  R  E  T  L  H  P  D  G  V  U
H  F  K  O  P  R  Y  O  J  J  N  U  A  W  M
B  I  F  E  C  Y  L  O  K  E  P  G  W  F  Y
S  L  U  V  Y  C  H  H  S  I  R  E  P  R  I
Y  E  U  E  V  N  Q  W  B  I  Q  M  R  L  J
T  E  W  R  W  S  X  C  O  N  D  E  M  N  B
Q  B  U  C  S  G  U  J  C  X  G  W  N  Q  T
W  A  N  O  R  B  C  S  P  H  R  H  R  I  U
```

For **GOD** so **LOVED** the world that he **GAVE** his one and
ONLY SON, that **WHOEVER BELIEVES** in him shall not
PERISH but have **ETERNAL LIFE**. For God did not **SEND**
his Son into the world to **CONDEMN** the **WORLD**, but to
SAVE the world through him.

JOHN 3:16–17

PSALM 23: FILL IN THE BLANK

Complete the Twenty-Third Psalm
using the King James Version.
Each blank holds one word.

The LORD is my (1)_____; I shall not want.

He maketh me to lie down in green (2)_____:

he leadeth me beside the still (3)_____.

He restoreth my soul: he leadeth me in the paths of

(4)_____ for his name's sake.

Yea, though I walk through the valley of the

(5)_____ of death, I will fear no

(6)_____: for thou art with me; thy rod and thy

staff they (7)_____ me.

Thou preparest a table before me in the presence of mine

(8)_____: thou anointest my head with oil; my

(9)_____ runneth over.

Surely goodness and mercy shall (10)_____ me

all the days of my life: and I will dwell in the house of the

(11)_____ for ever.

ALL THINGS BRIGHT AND BEAUTIFUL:
WORD SEARCH

*Cecil Frances Alexander (1818–1895)
wrote "All Things Bright and Beautiful"
as reflection on the phrase "Maker of
heaven and earth" from the Apostles'
Creed. Alexander based her hymn on
Genesis 1:31, with references to Matthew
8:28-29; Ecclesiastes 3:11; and Psalm 148.*

All things **BRIGHT** and **BEAUTIFUL**,
all **CREATURES** great and small,
all things **WISE** and **WONDERFUL**,
the Lord God made them all.

Each little **FLOWER** that opens,
each little **BIRD** that sings,
He made their glowing **COLORS**,
He made their tiny **WINGS**.

The purple-headed **MOUNTAIN**,
the **RIVER** running by,
the **SUNSET** and the **MORNING**
that brightens up the **SKY**.

The cold **WIND** in the **WINTER**,
the pleasant **SUMMER** sun,
the ripe **FRUITS** in the **GARDEN**:
He made them every one.

He gave us eyes to see them,
and **LIPS** that we might tell
how great is God **ALMIGHTY**,
who has made all things well.

Find the bolded words in the puzzle.
Words may be horizontal, vertical, or diagonal,
forward or backward, and may overlap.

```
L H R E M M U S I D F E Y E S O
B U S W O N D E R F U L C E L D
L I F V I B U M B W A N O M F N
W S O I M O R N I N G K I W E P
I G N H T R B N R G W C S D E P
A N O W T U R D H O W R P S R
N D I E Y E A C C L M A O J F R
U I T A R S Y E O H G S W D O H
A L O C T W F R B T O E I U R T
L C I R N N S A E R D R N P S A
M M N E W S U S S O R U D S A L
I K S V M A N O S K E T L T D P
G A P I S U B C M K Y A R I A R
H S W R S T M S P H D E F U P G
T J E S G N I W N U G R Y R O S
Y U L T H G I R B M S C O F C T
```

LANDS OF THE BIBLE TODAY: CROSSWORD

*The answers in this puzzle are Bible
locations one can still visit today.*

Across

2. Jesus healed a blind man by putting mud on his eyes and then telling him to bathe in this pool. (John 9:6–7)

5. Priests carrying the ark of the covenant stopped in the middle of this river to let all of Israel pass through. (Joshua 3:17)

6. In this valley, the evil Jezebel was devoured by dogs. (2 Kings 9:36)

7. Hometown of Philip, Andrew, and Peter. (John 1:44)

8. Town of David. (Luke 2:4)

10. Paul and Silas came here after they were asked to leave Philippi. (Acts 17:1)

11. Here Solomon built the temple on Mount Moriah. (2 Chronicles 3:1)

12. Where Lazarus, Mary, and Martha lived. (John 11:1)

13. Paul left his friends Priscilla and Aquila here. (Acts 18:19)

Down

1. The place of the skull. (Matthew 27:33)

3. Abraham made a treaty with Abimelek and Phicol here. (Genesis 21:32)

4. Goliath's homeland. (1 Samuel 17:4)

9. Here Jesus healed a paralyzed man who was lowered through the roof. (Mark 2:1–5)

11. Here Jonah boarded a ship heading for Tarshish. (Jonah 1:3)

RAISING OF LAZARUS:
WHAT GOES TOGETHER?

Read about the raising of Lazarus in John 11:1–44.

Using the following categories, create four groups of four terms that belong together.

Family Members

_____

_____

_____

_____

Words of Jesus

_____

_____

_____

_____

Titles of Jesus

_____

_____

_____

Lazarus's Tomb

_____

_____

_____

_____

Martha	Cave	Messiah	Rabbi
Lazarus, Come Out!	Sisters	Take Away the Stone	Stone
Mary	Teacher	I Am the Resurrection	Lord
Odor	Lazarus	Strips of Linen	You Will See the Glory of God

THE POWER OF WORDS:
FILL IN THE BLANK

*Complete the following verses
using the New International Version.
Each blank holds a single word.*

1. "The tongue has the power of _____ and _____." (Proverbs 18:21)

2. "A person finds _____ in giving an apt reply—and how good is a _____ word!" (Proverbs 15:23)

3. "Sin is not ended by _____ words, but the _____ hold their tongues." (Proverbs 10:19)

4. "The words of the mouth are deep _____, but the fountain of _____ is a rushing stream." (Proverbs 18:4)

5. "The mouths of _____ are their undoing, and their lips are a _____ to their very lives." (Proverbs 18:7)

6. "Let your conversation be always full of _____, seasoned with _____, so that you may know how to answer _____." (Colossians 4:6)

7. "Wounds from a friend can be _____, but an enemy multiplies _____." (Proverbs 27:6)

8. "Always be _____ to give an answer to everyone who asks you to give the reason for the _____ that you have. But do this with _____ and _____." (1 Peter 3:15)

Answer key on page 116.

THE POWER OF WORDS: WORD SEARCH

*In the puzzle below, find the words
you wrote in the blanks in THE POWER OF
WORDS: FILL IN THE BLANK.
Words may be horizontal, vertical, or diagonal,
forward or backward, and may overlap.*

```
V  P  N  Q  U  T  R  B  Y  S  U  E  S  S  E
J  A  G  G  C  O  U  D  C  L  A  S  Y  S  V
T  N  G  Y  C  S  T  U  U  Z  E  L  M  M  E
M  U  L  T  I  P  L  Y  I  N  G  M  T  N  R
V  V  D  V  X  O  J  T  E  P  A  K  I  P  Y
N  E  U  O  S  Q  R  L  K  D  O  B  Z  T  O
S  P  D  Z  V  U  T  T  G  V  M  O  Y  T  N
R  O  W  Y  S  N  H  J  Z  V  E  X  Y  L  E
E  H  A  T  E  M  X  P  M  Y  R  K  K  S  I
T  Z  E  G  O  Y  E  A  R  S  N  M  Y  V  A
A  D  X  D  Q  M  J  A  N  U  N  K  H  F  M
W  X  S  C  E  G  R  A  C  E  D  Y  O  J  F
D  I  X  J  Q  R  R  U  H  F  Z  E  Z  C  O
W  L  L  M  P  E  A  T  J  I  U  U  N  H  O
S  E  S  S  I  K  A  P  D  L  J  N  C  T  L
O  R  E  S  P  E  C  T  E  B  O  B  Q  X  S
D  W  A  N  D  F  L  C  Z  R  Q  J  Q  O  M
V  E  W  T  Q  Q  Y  E  I  S  P  D  P  P  C
```

*For further insight into the power of words,
read Proverbs 18 and James 3:1–12.*

COMMON SAYINGS FROM
THE OLD TESTAMENT: MATCHING

*Many phrases we still use
today are based on the Bible.
Match each missing word to its saying.*

A. BRIMSTONE   G. MOUTH
B. DUST   H. NOD
C. DUST   I. ORDER
D. FALL   J. SUN
E. KEEPER   K. TEETH
F. MATTER   L. WICKED

1. By the skin of your _____. (Job 19:20)

2. Ashes to ashes, dust to _____. (Genesis 3:19)

3. Am I my brother's _____? (Genesis 4:9)

4. The land of _____. (Genesis 4:16)

5. Fire and _____. (Psalm 11:6)

6. Put words in one's _____. (2 Samuel 14:3)

7. Put your house in _____. (Isaiah 38:1)

8. The root of the _____. (Job 19:28)

9. Bite the _____. (Psalm 72:9)

10. Pride comes before a _____.(Proverbs 16:18)

11. There's nothing new under the _____. (Ecclesiastes 1:9)

12. No peace for the _____. (Isaiah 57:21)

COMMON SAYINGS FROM
THE NEW TESTAMENT: MATCHING

*Many phrases we still use
today are based on the Bible.
Match each missing word to its saying.*

A. BLIND   G. LAW
B. CLOTHING   H. MILE
C. EARTH   I. NARROW
D. FAITH   J. PLATTER
E. FREE   K. SEPARATE
F. HEART   L. SWINE

1. Cast pearls before _____. (Matthew 7:6)

2. The blind leading the _____. (Matthew 15:13–14)

3. Straight and _____. (Matthew 7:14)

4. Wolves in sheep's _____. (Matthew 7:15)

5. Salt of the _____. (Matthew 5:13)

6. Letter of the _____. (2 Corinthians 3:6)

7. A man after my own _____. (Acts 13:22)

8. What God has joined together, let no one _____. (Matthew 19:6)

9. Head on a _____. (Mark 6:25)

10. O ye of little _____. (Luke 12:28)

11. The truth will set you _____. (John 8:32)

12. Go the extra _____. (Matthew 5:41)

CHRISTMAS STORY: WORD SEARCH

Words may be horizontal, vertical, or diagonal, forward or backward, and may overlap.

```
E  L  C  A  R  I  M  N  A  J  F  H  N  Q  S  S
M  S  G  N  I  D  I  T  H  Z  H  N  R  W  P  C
H  E  Y  G  U  Y  A  X  H  M  K  P  A  R  Q  T
F  Q  H  S  R  Z  J  T  A  G  A  D  N  M  Y  B
N  R  T  E  W  O  R  R  L  G  D  G  H  A  T  M
Y  B  A  B  L  I  Y  O  B  L  E  P  I  N  I  C
D  L  S  N  B  H  R  M  I  N  H  G  I  G  V  X
N  D  E  I  K  Y  T  N  W  N  T  A  K  E  I  E
C  I  V  U  F  I  G  E  P  I  O  B  U  R  T  T
B  L  G  R  N  A  S  B  L  R  R  P  Z  A  S
T  P  V  R  N  A  U  C  G  T  T  I  X  P  N  D
P  V  Q  G  I  S  M  C  E  K  E  E  D  L  O  G
H  L  E  W  E  V  E  M  C  N  B  L  H  W  O  J
D  L  I  J  D  W  I  K  I  X  S  X  V  V  Q  B
S  D  O  N  K  E  Y  T  J  O  S  E  P  H  U  T
S  H  E  P  H  E  R  D  S  U  Z  N  N  Q  L  U
```

ANGELS	GLORY	MARY
BABY	GOLD	MIRACLE
BETHLEHEM	IMMANUEL	MYRRH
BETROTHED	INN	NATIVITY
BIRTH	JESUS	SHEPHERDS
DONKEY	JOSEPH	SWADDLING
FRANKINCENSE	MAGI	TIDINGS
GABRIEL	MANGER	VIRGIN

PEOPLE KNOWN BY TWO NAMES:
WORD SCRAMBLE

*Each of the below people was known
by two names in Scripture. Unscramble
each person's other name.*

Old Name	New Name Scrambled	Unscramble
Abram (Genesis 17:5)	baahram	1. _____
Azariah (Daniel 1:7)	gdnebaoe	2. _____
Belteshazzar (Daniel 1:7)	naield	3. _____
Hananiah (Daniel 1:7)	hrdcshaa	4. _____
Israel (Genesis 32:28)	cajbo	5. _____
Jedidiah (2 Samuel 12:24–25)	sonooml	6. _____
Mishael (Daniel 1:7)	meachhs	7. _____
Sarai (Genesis 17:15)	hsaar	8. _____
Saul (Acts 13:9)	laup	9. _____
Simon (John 1:42)	epret	10. _____

MORE LANDS OF THE BIBLE TODAY: CROSSWORD

The answers in this puzzle are more Bible locations one can still visit today.

Across

2. The walls of this city were demolished with shouts and trumpet blasts. (Joshua 6:2)

4. Mount on which Elijah challenged the prophets of Baal to prove whose god was real. (1 Kings 18:19)

7. Village of Jesus's childhood. (Matthew 2:23)

8. Hannah's long prayed-for son, Samuel, was dedicated to the Lord at the temple in this city. (1 Samuel 1:24)

9. Paul landed in jail here for casting an evil spirit out of a slave girl. (Acts 16:12, 16–24)

11. Garden where Jesus prayed after the Last Supper. (Mark 14:32)

12. One of the cities King Solomon built. (1 Kings 9:15)

13. Jesus walked on this sea. (John 6:1)

Down

1. Joseph's bones were carried from Egypt and eventually buried here. (Joshua 24:32)

3. The mount Jesus will return to. (Zechariah 14:4)

5. Paul described the people of this city as lukewarm. (Revelation 3:14–16)

6. The king's palace from which Bathsheba was spied bathing. (2 Samuel 11:2–3)

10. Hometown of Mary, who had been cured of evil spirits. (Luke 8:2)

MUSICAL INSTRUMENTS
IN THE BIBLE: WORD SEARCH

*Words may be horizontal, vertical, or diagonal,
forward or backward, and may overlap.*

```
I  R  U  T  H  T  S  M  U  V  F  S  S  Y  T
I  U  F  G  I  G  F  O  L  U  G  L  L  R  P
N  N  W  S  M  M  R  D  X  N  A  A  M  E  A
L  N  R  R  E  Q  B  Q  I  B  H  U  R  T  Z
T  H  G  I  S  O  F  R  M  T  A  I  L  L  J
S  S  O  O  T  Z  T  Y  E  N  R  I  T  A  W
E  T  E  H  G  S  C  T  N  L  P  N  Q  S  S
H  P  E  C  X  O  E  R  Y  L  M  Z  P  P  H
L  L  I  N  I  J  N  M  Q  W  R  G  M  S  T
R  Q  F  P  A  O  T  G  B  Y  L  E  U  E  T
D  S  K  T  E  T  V  T  D  G  V  Y  K  H  R
H  Y  R  H  L  S  S  F  L  U  T  E  O  K  I
E  P  I  P  G  A  B  A  T  D  B  R  A  P  G
T  E  P  M  U  R  T  M  C  H  N  E  Z  E  O
S  Y  M  T  A  M  B  O  U  R  I  N  E  N  N
```

BAGPIPE	HARP	TIMBREL
CASTANETS	HORN	TRIGON
CHOIRS	LYRE	TRUMPET
CYMBALS	PSALTERY	VOICES
FLUTE	STRINGS	
GONG	TAMBOURINE	

*"Let everything that has breath praise the
LORD. Praise the LORD." —Psalm 150:6*

THE FRUIT OF THE SPIRIT IS . . . JOY

Complete the following verses about joy.
Each blank holds a single word.

1. "The joy of the LORD is your _____."
   (Nehemiah 8:10)

2. "I have no greater _____ than to hear that
   my children are walking in the _____."
   (3 John 1:4)

3. "If you keep my _____, you will remain in
   my love, just as I have kept my _____
   commands and remain in his love. I have told you this
   so that my joy may be in you and that your joy may be
   _____." (John 15:10–11)

4. "My lips will shout for joy when I sing _____ to
   you—I whom you have _____." (Psalm 71:23)

5. "Even though you do not see him now, you believe in
   him and are filled with an inexpressible and
   _____ joy, for you are receiving the end
   result of your faith, the _____ of your
   souls." (1 Peter 1:8–9)

6. "Now is your time of _____, but I will see
   you again and you will _____, and no one
   will take away your joy." (John 16:22)

7. "The prospect of the _____ is joy, but the
   hopes of the _____ come to nothing."
   (Proverbs 10:28)

To learn more about the fruit of the Spirit, read Galatians 5.

—— Answer key on page 119. ——

ISAIAH 40:28–31: FILL IN THE BLANK

*Complete the following verses
using the New International Version.
Each blank holds a single word.*

Do you not (1)_____?

    Have you not (2)_____?

The LORD is the (3)_____ God,

    the (4)_____ of the ends of the

    (5)_____.

He will not grow (6)_____ or

(7)_____,

    and his (8)_____ no one can fathom.

He gives (9)_____ to the weary

    and increases the (10)_____ of the weak.

Even youths grow (11)_____ and weary,

    and young men (12)_____ and fall;

but those who (13)_____ in the LORD

    will (14)_____ their strength.

They will soar on (15)_____ like

(16)_____;

    they will (17)_____ and not grow weary,

    they will (18)_____ and not be

    (19)_____.

(20)_____ 40:28–31

Answer key on page 119.

ISAIAH 40:28-31: WORD SEARCH

*In the puzzle below,
find the words you wrote in ISAIAH
40:28-31: FILL IN THE BLANK. Words
may be horizontal, vertical, or diagonal,
forward or backward, and may overlap.*

```
H  N  G  L  J  H  A  J  W  W  A  B  G  R  R
P  O  U  Z  S  T  T  E  B  V  O  N  H  E  E
N  E  P  R  I  I  A  G  F  C  I  N  D  W  N
N  J  A  E  V  R  V  F  N  T  Q  L  K  O  E
D  B  P  R  Y  E  T  H  S  E  K  Z  D  P  W
Y  W  Y  D  T  D  Z  A  N  D  R  Q  D  C  T
T  C  X  U  R  H  L  M  R  J  S  T  H  Z  W
A  Z  D  J  T  R  T  H  B  Z  P  D  S  M  S
O  I  R  S  E  L  G  A  E  J  E  G  F  K  J
S  B  A  V  X  T  E  G  V  R  N  H  E  K  J
C  K  E  V  N  K  R  T  I  P  G  R  J  S  U
E  M  H  I  W  R  S  T  U  M  B  L  E  N  I
G  N  A  I  S  A  I  A  H  J  Z  H  T  W  S
J  F  A  T  A  D  I  T  R  E  Q  A  I  K  X
G  N  I  D  N  A  T  S  R  E  D  N  U  L  A
C  R  E  A  T  O  R  B  R  A  G  Q  E  A  J
M  C  R  O  N  A  V  U  E  S  Y  R  B  W  J
I  D  O  D  F  E  B  E  T  A  C  I  P  V  H
```

PRIESTLY GARMENTS: MINI CROSS

*Insert the bolded words below
into the mini cross puzzle.*

These are the garments they
are to make: a **BREASTPIECE**,
an **EPHOD**, a **ROBE**, a woven
TUNIC, a **TURBAN** and a **SASH**.

Exodus 28:4

*To learn more about the materials and making of
Aaron's priestly garments, read Exodus 28.*

THE 7 I AMS OF JESUS: SCRIPTURE MATCH

*Match each "I Am" of Jesus with the
appropriate Scripture passage.*

I Am . . .

_____ 1. the bread of life

_____ 2. the gate

_____ 3. the good shepherd

_____ 4. the light of the world

_____ 5. the resurrection and the life

_____ 6. the true vine

_____ 7. the way, the truth, and the life

JOHN 6:35   JOHN 11:25
JOHN 8:12   JOHN 14:6
JOHN 10:9   JOHN 15:1
JOHN 10:11

*"'Very truly I tell you,' Jesus answered, 'before
Abraham was born, I am!'" —John 8:58*

HOLY, HOLY, HOLY: WORD SEARCH

*The lyrics of "Holy, Holy, Holy" were penned
by Reginald Heber (1783–1826). Heber
leaned heavily into the text of Revelation 4
and Isaiah 6:1–4 for this worshipful song.*

HOLY, Holy, Holy! Lord God **ALMIGHTY**!
Early in the **MORNING** our **SONG** shall rise to Thee.
Holy, Holy, Holy! **MERCIFUL** and **MIGHTY**!
God in three persons, **BLESSED TRINITY**!

Holy, Holy, Holy! All the **SAINTS ADORE** Thee,
Casting down their **GOLDEN CROWNS** around the
   GLASSY SEA;
CHERUBIM and **SERAPHIM** falling down before Thee,
Which wert and art and **EVERMORE** shall be.

Holy, Holy, Holy! Though the **DARKNESS** hide Thee,
Though the eye of sinful man Thy **GLORY** may not see,
Only Thou art holy; there is none beside Thee
PERFECT in pow'r, in **LOVE**, and **PURITY**.

Find the bolded words in the puzzle.
Words may be horizontal, vertical, or diagonal,
forward or backward, and may overlap.

```
M  O  H  S  D  M  G  H  G  N  D  Y  V  K  C
I  T  O  L  G  N  E  N  I  L  Q  W  L  H  Y
G  E  A  N  I  Q  W  R  A  J  B  Q  E  O  T
H  L  R  N  S  O  N  G  C  L  D  R  S  S  H
T  W  R  O  P  X  W  M  E  I  U  H  C  S  G
Y  O  T  R  M  B  S  S  U  B  F  N  L  E  I
M  E  U  K  O  R  S  T  I  P  K  U  I  N  M
I  L  C  R  O  E  E  M  N  N  B  L  K  L
O  Y  N  K  D  U  S  V  E  I  P  M  K  R  A
Y  T  I  N  I  R  T  D  E  B  A  Y  I  A  P
B  X  S  C  B  G  L  L  Y  B  A  S  Q  D  U
U  P  E  J  N  O  F  P  E  R  F  E  C  T  R
M  V  A  M  G  L  O  G  L  O  C  H  F  J  I
C  R  O  W  N  S  Y  E  L  L  X  R  D  V  T
Z  I  W  S  Y  R  E  R  T  A  O  G  E  H  Y
M  S  N  I  O  G  S  O  D  M  S  V  L  V  U
Y  L  F  L  E  R  Y  D  G  W  C  S  E  V  W
J  N  G  M  I  H  P  A  R  E  S  V  Y  J  N
```

OLD TESTAMENT
BIBLE SPOUSES: MATCHING

Match each person with his or her spouse.

1. Ruth (Ruth 4:9–10)

2. Eve (Genesis 3:20)

3. Hosea (Hosea 1:2–3)

4. Sarah (Genesis 17:15)

5. Moses (Exodus 2:21)

6. Rachel (Genesis 29:28)

7. Elkanah (1 Samuel 1:8)

8. Esther (Esther 2:16–17)

9. Jacob (Genesis 29)

10. Delilah (Judges 16:6)

11. Rebekah (Genesis 24:67)

12. David (2 Samuel 3:2–3)

_____Abigail

_____Abraham

_____Adam

_____Boaz

_____Gomer

_____Hannah

_____Isaac

_____Jacob

_____King Xerxes

_____Leah

_____Samson

_____Zipporah

MYSTERY: DOUBLE PUZZLE

Unscramble each word, then fill in the mystery phrase using the corresponding letters and numbers.

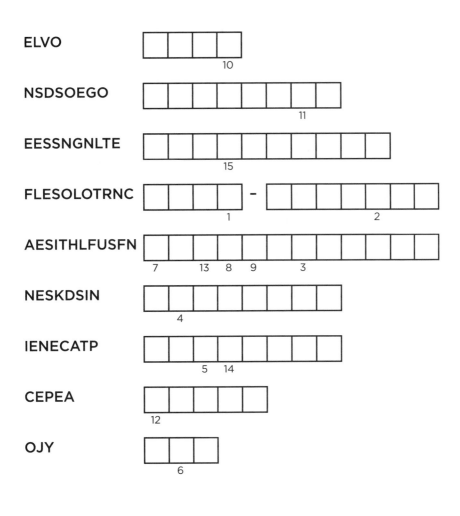

ELVO

NSDSOEGO

EESSNGNLTE

FLESOLOTRNC

AESITHLFUSFN

NESKDSIN

IENECATP

CEPEA

OJY

INSTRUCTION FOR PARENTS AND GRANDPARENTS: WORD SEARCH

Deuteronomy 6:1–2, 4–7 ESV

Now this is the **COMMANDMENT**—the **STATUTES** and the **RULES**—that the LORD your God commanded me to teach you, . . . that you may fear the **LORD** your God, you and your son and your son's **SON**, by keeping all his statutes and his commandments, which I command you, all the days of your **LIFE**, and that your days may be **LONG**.

HEAR, O Israel: The LORD our **GOD**, the LORD is one. You shall **LOVE** the LORD your God with all your **HEART** and with all your **SOUL** and with all your **MIGHT**. And these words that I command you today shall be on your heart. You shall **TEACH** them **DILIGENTLY** to your **CHILDREN**, and shall **TALK** of them when you **SIT** in your house, and when you **WALK** by the way, and when you **LIE** down, and when you **RISE**.

Find the bolded words in the puzzle.
Words may be horizontal, vertical, or diagonal,
forward or backward, and may overlap.

```
N  V  D  O  T  L  T  S  A  K  C  W  E  D  H
V  S  U  J  O  H  N  G  E  O  G  N  N  H  E
T  A  L  K  G  L  I  P  M  L  E  P  X  A  A
I  P  I  I  I  D  U  M  M  R  U  T  U  G  R
J  V  M  E  L  X  A  J  D  W  M  R  O  Q  D
T  E  A  C  H  N  N  L  N  A  L  D  H  Q  S
E  S  I  R  D  U  I  O  W  L  R  O  K  N  F
Y  E  V  M  H  H  S  F  S  K  O  C  N  B  L
O  H  E  E  C  R  Z  W  H  A  U  F  Z  G  U
T  N  S  E  T  U  T  A  T  S  O  W  V  E  O
T  R  Z  W  J  W  R  T  L  L  I  F  E  D  S
A  R  A  Y  L  T  N  E  G  I  L  I  D  R  U
S  M  B  E  V  I  B  H  J  I  T  F  A  O  O
Q  I  T  O  H  I  R  T  S  E  W  G  D  L  S
V  P  T  C  G  W  V  Y  R  L  E  V  O  L  F
```

JOSEPH SOLD INTO SLAVERY: WHAT GOES TOGETHER?

Read about Joseph and his brothers in Genesis 37.

Using the following categories, create four groups of four terms that belong together.

Joseph's Brothers

_____

_____

_____

_____

Dream Symbols

_____

_____

_____

Places

_____

_____

_____

_____

Merchant Goods

_____

_____

_____

_____

Sun	Canaan	Simeon	Moon
Myrrh	Dothan	Camels	Shechem
Reuben	Judah	Eleven Stars	Valley of Hebron
Balm	Spices	Benjamin	Sheaves of Grain

FISH TALES: CROSSWORD

Fishing was a common occupation and an important food source in the Bible. The following clues are related to fish and fishing.

Across

1. One of the eight gates in Jerusalem. (Zephaniah 1:10)
4. Number of fish Simon caught all night before Jesus got into his boat. (Luke 5:5)
7. Profession of Simon Peter and Andrew. (Matthew 4:18)
8. Jesus invited Simon Peter and Andrew to become fishers of these. (Luke 5:10)
9. One of Zebedee's sons. (See 9 down.) (Luke 5:10)
11. What Peter found in a fish's mouth. (Matthew 17:27)
12. Old Testament sea creature no fisherman would want to catch. (Psalm 104:26)
15. Disciple who dragged ashore net with 153 fish. (John 21:11)
16. Number of days Jonah was in belly of a fish. (Matthew 12:40)
17. Habakkuk complained that Judah's enemies caught their people as though using this device. (Habakkuk 1:12–15)

Down

2. A loving father would not give a son this. (Luke 11:11)
3. Before Jesus's ascension to heaven, he ate fish prepared this way. (Luke 24:42)
5. After Jesus's resurrection, he cooked this. (John 21:12–13)
6. Day that fish and fowl were created. (Genesis 1:20–23)
9. One of Zebedee's sons. (See 9 across.) (Luke 5:10)
10. Simon Peter and Andrew were fishing in this sea. (Mark 1:16)
13. In a prophecy about Egypt, fishermen who throw their hooks into this river will groan and lament. (Isaiah 19:8)
14. Prophet swallowed by a huge fish. (Jonah 1:17)
16. Number of fish at feeding of 5,000 men. (Luke 9:16)

THE FRUIT OF THE SPIRIT IS . . . PEACE: MULTIPLE CHOICE

Choose the correct answer.

1. Which part of the armor of God is associated with peace? (Ephesians 6:15)

   a. Gauntlets

   b. Helmet

   c. Breastplate

   d. Shoes

2. Which of the horsemen in Revelation was given the power to take peace from the earth? (Revelation 6:4)

   a. The rider of the white horse

   b. The rider of the red horse

   c. The rider of the black horse

   d. The rider of the pale horse

3. How did the Gibeonites trick Joshua into making a peace treaty with them? (Joshua 9:6)

   a. They pretended to be from a distant country, far away from the promised land.

   b. They manned their walls with straw soldiers to give a false impression of their numbers.

   c. They offered to lead the Israelites through the canyons to ambush other Canaanite cities.

   d. They produced a miracle using their secret arts, claiming it was a sign from heaven that the two nations should make peace.

4. Because David was not a man of peace and rest, God did not allow him to (1 Chronicles 22:8–9):

   a. Defeat the Amalekites

   b. Build the temple

   c. Bring the ark of the covenant to Jerusalem

   d. Offer sacrifices

5. Jesus said, "Blessed are the peacemakers, for . . ." (Matthew 5:9)

   a. they will inherit the earth.

   b. theirs is the kingdom of heaven.

   c. they will be called children of God.

   d. they will be comforted.

MAHERSHALALHASHBAZ: ARRANGE THE LETTERS

Mahershalalhashbaz is the longest name in the Bible. The son of the Old Testament prophet Isaiah and "the prophetess," God named this child even before he was conceived. His name means "quick to the plunder, swift to the spoil."* The meaning of his name points to the impending pillaging of Samaria and Damascus by Assyria. Not much more is known of Mahershalalhashbaz except for the quick mentions in Isaiah 8:1–4.

How many words of 3 or more letters can you make from the name

MAHERSHALALHASHBAZ

Use each letter only once per word.

_____ _____ _____

_____ _____ _____

_____ _____ _____

_____ _____ _____

_____ _____ _____

_____ _____ _____

_____ _____ _____

_____

* Derived from NIV note for Isaiah 1:8.

BUT GOD . . . NEW TESTAMENT VERSES: FILL IN THE BLANK

Using the word bank,
fill in one word per blank.

1. "Jesus looked at them and said to them, 'With men this is impossible, *but with God* all things are _____.'" (Matthew 19:26 NKJV)

2. "And when they had carried out all that was written of him, they took him down from the tree and laid him in a tomb. *But God* raised him from the _____." (Acts 13:29–30 ESV)

3. "I planted, Apollos watered, *but God* gave the _____." (1 Corinthians 3:6 ESV)

4. "No temptation has overtaken you except such as is common to man; *but God* is faithful, who will not allow you to be _____ beyond what you are able." (1 Corinthians 10:13 NKJV)

5. "We all once lived in the passions of our flesh, . . . and were by nature children of wrath, like the rest of mankind. *But God*, being rich in _____ . . . made us alive together with Christ." (Ephesians 2:3–5 ESV)

6. "I am suffering even to the point of being chained like a criminal. *But God's word* is not _____." (2 Timothy 2:9)

A. CHAINED
B. DEAD
C. GROWTH

D. MERCY
E. POSSIBLE
F. TEMPTED

The God of the Bible is still God. When our circumstances seem too difficult to straighten out or overcome, we can read Scripture and ponder the truth: But God . . .

44

—— Answer key on page 124. ——

BOOKS OF THE BIBLE NAMED AFTER A PERSON—OLD TESTAMENT: WORD SEARCH

*Words may be horizontal, vertical, or diagonal,
forward or backward, and may overlap.*

```
B  K  C  L  N  S  S  R  I  N  S  Y  H  K  Z  H
N  B  J  B  E  Y  T  O  U  T  A  A  R  Y  L  A
I  Z  O  T  B  Z  H  R  M  T  I  H  H  U  O  I
H  A  I  M  E  H  E  N  E  A  H  O  U  Z  U  D
A  M  G  L  V  T  V  K  S  H  S  K  S  M  C  A
B  C  H  G  W  I  B  I  I  E  T  L  E  O  J  B
A  I  A  F  A  I  O  H  A  E  B  S  Z  V  V  O
K  D  I  S  H  H  J  H  Z  C  L  T  E  L  Y  B
K  A  R  H  Z  C  A  J  E  R  E  M  I  A  H  A
U  N  A  S  S  N  S  S  Z  Z  N  U  C  L  I  D
K  I  H  O  O  H  A  P  R  R  L  A  P  H  O  I
L  E  C  J  R  J  M  A  A  G  U  I  C  H  K  A
Y  L  E  T  C  Z  U  H  A  I  N  A  H  P  E  Z
S  M  Z  T  D  E  E  C  M  Y  L  O  Q  I  O  P
O  B  B  Z  I  Z  L  N  Q  A  A  M  I  C  A  H
J  O  S  H  U  A  U  A  M  H  S  A  S  Y  G  C
```

JOSHUA	JOB	JOEL	HABAKKUK
RUTH	ISAIAH	AMOS	ZEPHANIAH
SAMUEL	JEREMIAH	OBADIAH	HAGGAI
EZRA	EZEKIEL	JONAH	ZECHARIAH
NEHEMIAH	DANIEL	MICAH	MALACHI
ESTHER	HOSEA	NAHUM	

GREAT IS THY FAITHFULNESS: WORD SEARCH

"Great Is Thy Faithfulness" was written, along with twelve hundred other poems, by Thomas O. Chisholm (1866–1960). Inspired by the simple, daily provisions of God in his life, Chisholm penned this hymn based on Lamentations 3:22–23.

Great is Thy **FAITHFULNESS**, O God my Father;
there is no **SHADOW** of turning with Thee;
Thou changest not, Thy **COMPASSIONS**, they fail not;
as Thou hast been, Thou forever wilt be.

GREAT is Thy faithfulness!
Great is Thy faithfulness!
Morning by morning new **MERCIES** I see;
all I have needed Thy hand hath **PROVIDED**:
great is Thy faithfulness, Lord, unto me!

Summer and winter, and **SPRINGTIME** and **HARVEST**;
sun, moon, and **STARS** in their courses above
join with all **NATURE** in manifold **WITNESS**
to Thy great faithfulness, mercy, and love.

PARDON for sin and a peace that endureth,
Thine own dear **PRESENCE** to cheer and to guide;
STRENGTH for today and bright **HOPE** for tomorrow:
BLESSINGS all mine, with ten **THOUSAND** beside!

Find the bolded words in the puzzle.
Words may be horizontal, vertical, or diagonal,
forward or backward, and may overlap.

```
P  A  R  S  S  E  L  M  G  C  I  S  S  N  A  S
U  M  E  L  G  H  A  R  F  E  C  H  E  O  T  E
R  E  V  E  R  O  F  I  F  O  L  A  I  D  U  E
S  P  R  I  N  G  T  I  M  E  D  D  C  R  C  N
F  U  T  U  J  L  N  P  C  E  N  O  R  A  O  W
E  A  R  A  H  M  A  W  D  V  U  W  E  P  E  D
S  H  I  O  E  S  T  I  L  R  B  P  M  R  M  S
T  S  P  T  S  R  V  H  S  E  R  U  T  A  N  T
D  E  E  I  H  O  G  E  A  D  M  I  R  F  I  R
N  P  O  N  R  F  S  M  P  R  E  S  E  N  C  E
A  N  S  P  T  A  U  N  E  W  V  O  N  O  U  N
S  I  T  A  Y  I  N  L  A  R  D  E  G  N  J  G
U  T  A  I  T  V  W  E  N  A  W  R  S  T  U  T
O  Y  R  S  G  N  I  S  S  E  L  B  E  T  U  H
H  I  S  T  B  S  H  O  S  N  S  R  P  U  Y  D
T  R  E  B  H  T  G  N  E  S  G  S  N  F  U  L
```

PARABLE OF THE PRODIGAL SON: WHAT GOES TOGETHER?

Read the parable of the prodigal son in Luke 15:11–32.

Using the following categories, create four groups of four terms that belong together.

The Father's Inheritance

_____

_____

_____

_____

The Father's Response

_____

_____

_____

_____

In a Distant Country

_____

_____

_____

_____

Symbols of the Father's Favor

_____

_____

_____

_____

Pigs	Fattened Calf	Wealth	Wild Living
Running	Estate	Kiss	Famine
Sandals	Ring	Pods	Property
Compassion	Share	Hug	Robe

MONEY: CROSSWORD

Did you know that over 2,000 Bible verses talk about money and possessions? To review a few of these verses, complete this puzzle using the English Standard Version.

Across

2. "Honor the LORD with your _____, and with the firstfruits of all your produce." (Proverbs 3:9)

3. "It is more _____ to give than to receive." (Acts 20:35)

5. Jesus commended a widow for putting two very small copper _____ in the temple treasury. (Mark 12:41–44)

6. "Do not lay up for yourselves _____ on earth." (Matthew 6:19)

9. In Jesus's parable, the unmerciful servant owed his master ten thousand of these. (Matthew 18:24)

11. "Whoever trusts in his riches will fall, but the righteous will _____ like a green leaf." (Proverbs 11:28)

13. "Where your treasure is, there will your _____ be also." (Luke 12:34)

14. "You cannot _____ both God and money." (Matthew 6:24)

Down

1. "The righteous is _____ and gives." (Psalm 37:21)

4. "Do not _____ money . . . be content with your wages." (Luke 3:14)

7. The early believers shared _____ in common. (Acts 4:32)

8. "He who loves money will not be _____ with money." (Ecclesiastes 5:10)

10. "Whoever oppresses the _____ to increase his own wealth, or gives to the rich, will only come to poverty." (Proverbs 22:16)

12. Micah and other prophets criticized the people of Israel for using this dishonest measuring tool. (Micah 6:11)

15. "The love of money is a ____ of all kinds of evils." (1 Timothy 6:10)

51

BOOKS OF THE NEW TESTAMENT: WORD SEARCH

Words may be horizontal, vertical, or diagonal, forward or backward, and may overlap.

```
R  A  M  W  E  H  T  T  A  M  K  N  U  W  H
T  O  H  N  S  L  M  V  G  C  H  R  S  F  E
R  K  M  S  R  O  H  A  O  O  N  U  A  G  B
S  E  R  A  N  O  L  V  J  R  T  R  J  M  R
E  N  T  K  N  A  S  N  A  I  S  E  H  P  E
K  H  X  E  T  S  I  D  T  N  C  G  T  Y  W
U  O  E  I  P  X  I  P  S  T  I  W  E  H  S
L  J  A  S  E  M  A  J  P  H  A  L  I  T  V
K  N  Z  C  O  L  O  S  S  I  A  N  S  O  F
S  P  H  I  L  E  M  O  N  A  L  G  R  M  U
R  E  V  E  L  A  T  I  O  N  S  I  E  I  Y
F  S  N  A  I  N  O  L  A  S  S  E  H  T  X
B  R  D  A  C  T  S  W  J  U  D  E  D  P  S
```

MATTHEW	(1 & 2) THESSALONIANS
MARK	(1 & 2) TIMOTHY
LUKE	TITUS
JOHN	PHILEMON
ACTS	HEBREWS
ROMANS	JAMES
(1 & 2) CORINTHIANS	(1 & 2) PETER
GALATIANS	(1, 2, & 3) JOHN
EPHESIANS	JUDE
PHILIPPIANS	REVELATION
COLOSSIANS	

"Your word is truth." —John 17:17 NKJV

——— *Answer key on page 127.* ———

THE ARK OF THE COVENANT: MINI CROSS

Exodus 25:10–22 describes the construction of the ark of the covenant in great detail. Insert these ark components into the mini cross puzzle.

ACACIA   GOLD   RINGS
CHERUBIM   POLES   WINGS

To find out what items the ark of the covenant contained, read Hebrews 9:3–4.

"Then the temple of God was opened in heaven, and the ark of His covenant was seen in His temple. And there were lightnings, noises, thunderings, an earthquake, and great hail." —Revelation 11:19 NKJV

NUMBERS IN THE BIBLE:
FILL IN THE BLANK

Fill in each blank with an answer from the number bank. Each quoted Scripture in this puzzle is from the New King James Version.

a. "Again David gathered all the choice men of Israel, _____." (2 Samuel 6:1)

b. Peter miraculously caught _____ large fish when Jesus appeared to him after His resurrection. (John 21:11)

c. Methuselah was _____ years old when he died. (Genesis 5:27)

d. "And the LORD said, 'My Spirit shall not strive with man forever, for he is indeed flesh; yet his days shall be _____ years.'" (Genesis 6:3)

e. On the day of Pentecost, approximately _____ people accepted Peter's message about Jesus Christ. (Acts 2:41)

f. Jesus fed about _____ men, besides women and children, with only five loaves of bread and two fish. (Matthew 14:21)

g. Samson killed _____ Philistine men with the jawbone of a donkey. (Judges 15:15–16)

h. Solomon married _____ wives of royal birth, not including concubines. (1 Kings 11:3)

i. Jesus appeared to more than _____ people after His resurrection. (1 Corinthians 15:6)

j. Aaron the high priest was _____ years old when he died. (Numbers 33:39)

k. The book of Psalms has _____ chapters.

l. _____ people from all the tribes of Israel were sealed by the four angels. (Revelation 7:4)

m. An angel measured the new Jerusalem and found it to be _____ furlongs (about 1,400 miles or 2,200 kilometers) in width, length, and height. (Revelation 21:16)

n. Abraham lived to be _____ years old. (Genesis 25:7)

o. The number of the beast is _____. (Revelation 13:18)

p. Lamech lived to be _____ years old, and then he died. (Genesis 5:31)

q. _____ people were killed in a severe earthquake during the second woe of John's Revelation. (Revelation 11:13)

r. The woman fled to the wilderness to be taken care of by God for _____ days. (Revelation 12:6)

Number Bank

120	500	1,000	12,000
123	666	1,260	30,000
150	700	3,000	144,000
153	777	5,000	
175	969	7,000	

———— Answer key on page 128. ————

HEROES OF THE BIBLE: WORD SEARCH

*Words may be horizontal, vertical, or diagonal,
forward or backward, and may overlap.*

```
S  A  M  S  O  N  D  E  B  E  O  H  P  U  G  I
A  Z  I  O  E  A  I  A  C  E  D  R  O  M  I  O
R  H  C  D  N  S  H  A  I  K  E  Z  E  H  D  Y
A  L  A  I  Y  V  O  Y  H  B  J  V  O  D  E  J
H  Z  E  R  N  L  X  M  Z  A  R  O  B  E  O  S
A  L  E  H  O  U  D  I  V  A  D  I  S  S  N  H
B  B  S  S  C  B  O  I  J  H  F  L  I  E  A  J
O  P  R  N  T  A  E  F  O  T  D  A  U  G  P  P
C  A  P  A  Y  H  R  D  S  R  H  L  A  H  E  H
A  U  V  R  H  N  E  F  H  A  H  R  U  T  L  B
J  L  A  L  H  A  O  R  U  M  A  H  E  E  W  A
O  M  I  R  I  A  M  A  A  A  J  R  A  D  H  H
E  L  I  Z  A  B  B  T  H  N  I  J  U  S  O  A
D  E  A  B  I  G  A  I  L  N  L  N  I  T  I  R
N  E  H  E  M  I  H  H  W  A  E  L  J  O  H  N
R  E  B  E  K  A  H  E  C  W  E  H  A  E  L  L
```

ABIGAIL	HAGAR	LYDIA	RACHEL
ABRAHAM	HEZEKIAH	MARTHA	RAHAB
ANNA	HULDAH	MARY	REBEKAH
DANIEL	JACOB	MIRIAM	RUTH
DAVID	JAEL	MORDECAI	SAMSON
DEBORAH	JOHN	MOSES	SARAH
ELIJAH	JOSEPH	NOAH	
ELISHA	JOSHUA	PAUL	
ESTHER	JOSIAH	PETER	
GIDEON	LEAH	PHOEBE	

THE LIFE OF DAVID: WORD SEARCH

*Words may be horizontal, vertical, or diagonal,
forward or backward, and may overlap.*

```
L  N  A  T  H  A  N  A  S  C  G  L  H  N  U  J
R  E  H  V  R  Y  P  N  L  X  E  U  Y  I  U  J
M  B  U  M  U  O  X  O  I  G  X  A  S  A  O  P
O  E  O  M  M  U  A  I  N  E  N  S  Y  N  O  H
M  R  H  V  A  E  H  N  G  O  L  I  A  T  H  I
J  A  B  E  H  S  H  T  A  B  B  T  K  H  T  L
Z  E  S  L  L  X  N  E  C  A  H  E  H  U  Z  I
P  C  R  H  E  H  B  D  I  A  H  R  X  J  W  S
R  P  A  U  E  P  T  L  N  A  T  Y  G  E  A  T
K  A  F  A  S  P  L  E  H  F  N  L  T  S  R  I
E  S  E  A  B  A  H  A  B  C  A  I  H  S  R  N
N  W  L  P  H  S  L  E  N  J  N  Q  W  E  I  E
O  M  J  C  S  E  A  E  R  S  E  B  O  R  O  S
T  U  I  I  R  T  Y  L  M  D  V  S  W  O  R  D
S  M  V  N  O  M  O  L  O  S  O  H  A  D  U  J
A  B  I  G  A  I  L  H  S  M  C  V  J  C  U  X
```

ABIGAIL	JONATHAN	SAMUEL
ABSALOM	JUDAH	SAUL
ANOINTED	KING	SHEPHERD
ARMOR	LYRE	SLING
BATHSHEBA	MICHAL	SOLOMON
COVENANT	NATHAN	SPEAR
ELAH	PHILISTINES	STONE
GOLIATH	PSALM	SWORD
JESSE	ROBE	WARRIOR

BIBLE PROFESSIONS: CROSSWORD

*Fill in the puzzle with the professions
of the people in the clues.*

Across

5. Tubal Cain (Genesis 4:22)

6. Lydia (Acts 16:14)

7. Ethiopian eunuch (Acts 8:27)

10. Cornelius (Acts 10:1)

13. Joseph's prison mate reinstated by Pharaoh (Genesis 40:21)

15. Priscilla and Aquila (Acts 18:1–3)

17. Simon (Acts 9:43)

18. Amos (Amos 1:1)

20. Joseph's prison mate executed by Pharaoh (Genesis 40:22)

21. Nimrod (Genesis 10:9)

22. Simon Peter (Luke 5:2–3)

Down

1. Nebuchadnezzar (2 Kings 24:1)

2. Ezra (Ezra 7:6 ESV)

3. Cain (Genesis 4:2)

4. Joseph, son of Jacob (Genesis 42:6)

8. Demetrius (Acts 19:24)

9. Dorcas (Acts 9:39)

11. Joseph, the husband of Mary (Matthew 13:55)

12. Moses (Deuteronomy 34:10)

14. Jezebel (1 Kings 16:29–31)

16. Ezekiel (Ezekiel 1:3)

19. Luke (Colossians 4:14)

"Commit your work to the LORD." —*Proverbs 16:3 ESV*

THE FRUIT OF THE SPIRIT IS . . .
KINDNESS: WORD SCRAMBLE

*Unscramble the bolded words
in the verses below.*

1. _____: "Praise be to the LORD, the God of
   my master Abraham, who has not abandoned his
   kindness and **INAFFLESTHUS** to my master." (Genesis
   24:27)

2. _____: "While Joseph was there in the
   prison, the LORD was with him; he showed him
   kindness and granted him **OVFRA** in the eyes of the
   prison warden." (Genesis 39:20–21)

3. _____: "Our God has not **NASKOFER** us in
   our bondage. He has shown us kindness in the sight of
   the kings of Persia: He has granted us new life." (Ezra
   9:9)

4. _____: "Anyone who **SHLOWDITH**
   kindness from a friend forsakes the fear of the
   Almighty." (Job 6:14)

5. _____: "Let a **STROUHIGE** man strike me—
   that is a kindness; let him rebuke me—that is oil on my
   head." (Psalm 141:5)

6. _____: "'With **GALERVETSIN** kindness I will
   have compassion on you,' says the LORD." (Isaiah 54:8)

7. _____: "I will tell of the kindnesses of the
   LORD . . . yes, the many good things he has done for
   Israel, according to his **SPASMICOON** and many
   kindnesses." (Isaiah 63:7)

8. _____: "I am the LORD, who exercises kindness, **SUIJECT** and righteousness on earth." (Jeremiah 9:24)

9. _____: "I led them with **SROCD** of human kindness, with ties of love. To them I was like one who lifts a little child to the cheek, and I bent down to feed them." (Hosea 11:4)

10. _____: "He has shown kindness by giving you rain from heaven and crops in their seasons; he **DRESIVOP** you with plenty of food and fills your hearts with joy." (Acts 14:17)

11. _____: "The islanders showed us unusual kindness. They built a fire and **CLEMODEW** us all because it was raining and cold." (Acts 28:2)

12. _____: "Do you show contempt for the riches of his kindness, forbearance and **APENICTE**, not realizing that God's kindness is intended to lead you to repentance?" (Romans 2:4)

13. _____: "God raised us up with Christ . . . , in order that in the coming ages he might show the incomparable riches of his **CREGA**, expressed in his kindness to us." (Ephesians 2:6–7)

14. _____: "When the kindness and love of God our Savior appeared, he saved us, not because of righteous things we had done, but because of his **CRYME**." (Titus 3:4–5)

Answer key on page 130.

THE FRUIT OF THE SPIRIT IS . . .
FAITHFULNESS: WORD SEARCH

*Find the words related to God's faithfulness,
as described throughout Scripture.
Words may be horizontal, vertical, or diagonal,
forward or backward, and may overlap.*

```
S  S  E  N  D  O  L  F  A  N  M  E  R  O  B  E
A  U  F  L  W  E  O  P  O  R  E  F  U  G  P  V
L  N  O  M  O  R  N  I  D  G  R  U  C  A  G  E
V  A  L  I  E  V  S  D  E  N  C  E  T  I  C  R
A  H  U  V  C  S  E  G  U  T  Y  I  B  I  T  L
T  R  E  P  A  A  U  S  C  R  E  D  T  G  C  A
I  R  T  P  O  F  R  T  I  N  E  S  U  N  E  S
O  S  M  E  E  F  I  G  T  M  U  S  P  I  T  T
N  O  N  R  D  O  O  G  A  J  O  S  T  L  O  I
C  H  A  K  I  N  D  N  E  S  S  R  D  I  R  N
D  E  D  I  V  I  D  N  U  P  R  I  P  A  P  G
A  C  O  V  E  N  A  N  T  E  V  E  R  F  O  R
D  U  P  R  I  G  H  T  E  O  U  S  E  N  G  I
J  U  S  T  N  E  S  O  U  S  A  L  P  U  B  O
E  C  A  E  P  A  S  S  I  O  K  N  O  D  A  S
N  I  O  T  E  N  D  U  L  I  A  F  H  R  C  Y
```

COMPASSION	GRACIOUS	PATIENT	SALVATION
COVENANT	HOPE	PEACE	UNDIVIDED
ENDURES	JUSTICE	PROMISE	UNFAILING
EVERLASTING	KINDNESS	PROTECT	UPRIGHT
FOREVER	LOVE	REFUGE	
GOOD	MERCY	RIGHTEOUS	

—— *Answer key on page 130.* ——

THE FRUIT OF THE SPIRIT IS . . .
GOODNESS: WORD SEARCH

*Find the words related to God's goodness,
as described throughout Scripture.
Words may be horizontal, vertical, or diagonal,
forward or backward, and may overlap.*

```
B L E E S G H L B A T E G N A M
T S A L T O E L I N O N U R B A
O R M I N N A N E G I A N L U H
L T U E T M N M E V H P I U N O
L E S T E R G O I R M T T F D L
E T I L H D A G I E O F Y H A Y
D R E S U F R P R S P U F T N A
I S T J L O U C M T S L S I T S
S O N U F L Y L S I N A M A L D
H D E S S E L B E C A E P F U L
L I C T F R U I T F U L O M J U
O G O J U S T I C E N T L Y O J
V I N M O D S I W L E S S I N C
E L N T S E N O P E L B M U H A
N O I S T R U S H F I A T H E R
A S E L F C O N T R O L A E D E
```

ABUNDANT	FRUITFUL	INNOCENT	PEACE
BLAMELESS	GENEROUS	JUDGMENT	SELF-CONTROL
BLESSED	HOLY	JUSTICE	TRUTHFUL
COMPASSION	HONEST	LIGHT	UNITY
FAITHFUL	HUMBLE	LOVE	WISDOM
FORGIVING	IMPARTIAL	MERCY	

*"O give thanks unto the LORD; for he is good: for
his mercy endureth for ever." —Psalm 136:1 KJV*

Answer key on page 131.

THE FRUIT OF THE SPIRIT IS . . .
GENTLENESS: WORD SCRAMBLE

*Unscramble the bolded words
in the below verses.*

1. _____: "After the earthquake came a fire, but the LORD was not in the fire. And after the fire came a gentle **PRISHEW**." (1 Kings 19:12–13)

2. _____: "Can you pull in Leviathan with a fishhook or tie down its tongue with a rope? . . . Will it keep begging you for **ECRYM**? Will it speak to you with gentle words?" (Job 41:1, 3)

3. _____: "A gentle answer turns away **TRAWH**, but a harsh word stirs up anger." (Proverbs 15:1)

4. _____: "Through **EPECINTA** a ruler can be persuaded, and a gentle tongue can break a bone." (Proverbs 25:15)

5. _____: "Take my yoke upon you and learn from me, for I am gentle and **MELBUH** in heart, and you will find rest for your souls." (Matthew 11:29)

6. _____: "Say to Daughter Zion, 'See, your **GINK** comes to you, gentle and riding on a donkey.'" (Matthew 21:5)

7. _____: "What do you prefer? Shall I come to you with a rod of discipline, or shall I come in love and with a gentle **PRISTI**?" (1 Corinthians 4:21)

8. _____: "By the **LITHYMUI** and gentleness of Christ, I appeal to you." (2 Corinthians 10:1)

9. _____: "Be completely humble and gentle; be patient, **IGREBAN** with one another in love." (Ephesians 4:2)

10. _____: "Let your gentleness be **TENDIVE** to all. The Lord is near." (Philippians 4:5)

11. _____: "Clothe yourselves with compassion, **DISNNESK**, humility, gentleness and patience." (Colossians 3:12)

12. _____: "Now the overseer is to be above reproach, . . . not **LINTOVE** but gentle, not quarrelsome, not a lover of money." (1 Timothy 3:2–3)

13. _____: "Flee from all this, and pursue righteousness, **ESLODSING**, faith, love, endurance and gentleness." (1 Timothy 6:11)

14. _____: "Remind the people to . . . be **CLEEPABEA** and considerate, and always to be gentle toward everyone." (Titus 3:1–2)

15. _____: "Your beauty should . . . be that of your inner self, the unfading beauty of a gentle and **TIQUE** spirit." (1 Peter 3:3–4)

16. _____: "Always be prepared to give an answer to everyone who asks you to give the reason for the hope that you have. But do this with gentleness and **SCREEPT**." (1 Peter 3:15)

THE LIFE & DEMISE OF JUDAS: CROSSWORD

Across

3. Judas's father. (John 6:71)

5. After the Last Supper, Jesus and the disciples went to the Mount of _____. (Matthew 26:30)

6. Overcome with remorse, Judas threw his money here. (Matthew 27:5)

10. Title Judas used to address Jesus. (Matthew 26:49)

13. It would have been better if Jesus's betrayer had never been _____. (Matthew 26:24)

14. Epithet often used to describe Judas. (Matthew 26:14)

15. Field where Judas hanged himself. (Matthew 27:8)

17. Garden where Judas betrayed Jesus. (Matthew 26:36)

19. Judas betrayed Jesus for _____ pieces of silver. (Matthew 26:14–15)

20. Judas was keeper of the _____ for the disciples. (John 12:6)

Down

1. Jesus describes Judas as a _____. (John 6:70)

2. Jesus was arrested by men armed with _____ and clubs. (Matthew 26:47)

4. On the night he was betrayed, Jesus took a cup and said, "This is my blood of the _____." (Matthew 26:28 ESV)

7. The chief priests could not put Judas's silver coins into the treasury because they were _____ _____. (Matthew 27:6)

8. After his betrayal, Jesus was questioned by the _____. (Matthew 26:59)

9. Jesus was brought before this high priest. (Matthew 26:57)

11. Jesus identified his betrayer with a piece of _____. (John 13:26)

12. Jesus and the disciples were celebrating this before Jesus was betrayed. (Matthew 26:17)

16. The field where Judas hanged himself was later used as a burial place for _____. (Matthew 27:7)

18. The apostle chosen to replace Judas. (Acts 1:23–26)

SWING LOW, SWEET CHARIOT: WORD SEARCH

One of the best-known African American spirituals, "Swing Low, Sweet Chariot" was widely popularized by the Fisk Jubilee Singers and the Hampton Singers. The song borrows the imagery of the Jordan River and the chariot from the account of Elijah's ascent to heaven in 2 Kings 2.

Swing **LOW**, sweet **CHARIOT**,
coming for to carry me home.
SWING low, **SWEET** chariot,
coming for to carry me home.

I looked over **JORDAN**, and what did I see,
coming for to carry me home.
A **BAND** of **ANGELS** coming after me,
coming for to carry me **HOME**.

If you get there **BEFORE** I do,
coming for to carry me home.
Tell all my **FRIENDS** I'm coming too,
coming for to **CARRY** me home.

The **BRIGHTEST** day that ever I saw,
coming for to carry me home.
When **JESUS WASHED** my **SINS** away,
coming for to carry me home.

I'm **SOMETIMES** up and sometimes **DOWN**,
coming for to carry me home.
But still my **SOUL** feels **HEAVENLY BOUND**,
COMING for to carry me home.

Find the bolded words in the puzzle.
Words may be horizontal, vertical, or diagonal,
forward or backward, and may overlap.

```
T D S W E E D O E H S C A G N I
U S N O U B O M D I H W B N H E
N W E U M A W T H A N F E I S O
R S A T O E N G R M A D F M U L
U N T R H B T I S H D B O O N E
G E W R A G O I N T R I R C A T
S U I L A T I P M E O H E A R E
G N I W S M E R O E J S O H U L
S D N E I R F D B N S U D M E S
J E F S D N E E H L F S Y B E W
N D O Y C H T D L O N E W A S M
B U P A S Y N E M W U J O N H S
L H R A H A J C E H I U S V K Y
A R W E B R O I B W A N G E L S
Y L N E V A E H S U S Y B T O J
S I N S G I V A P I R A S O M E
```

JOHN THE BAPTIST: CROSSWORD

"John the Baptist appeared in the wilderness, preaching a baptism of repentance for the forgiveness of sins." —Mark 1:4

Across

4. Name of the angel who foretold John's birth. (Luke 1:19)

5. How John the Baptist was executed. (Matthew 14:10)

8. John the Baptist fulfilled this prophet's words. (Matthew 3:3)

9. John's father. (Luke 1:13)

13. John the Baptist's belt was made of this material. (Matthew 3:4)

15. Jesus compares John the Baptist to this Old Testament prophet. (Matthew 11:14)

16. This is what Herod was celebrating on the day he executed John the Baptist. (Matthew 14:6)

17. John the Baptist ate these insects. (Matthew 3:4)

19. The man who put John in prison. (Matthew 14:3)

20. Jesus said he needed to be baptized in order to _____ all righteousness. (Matthew 3:15)

Down

1. John the Baptist preached in this wilderness. (Matthew 3:1)

2. John called the Pharisees and Sadducees a brood of _____. (Matthew 3:7)

3. Where Jesus came from to be baptized by John. (Matthew 3:13)

6. John's mother. (Luke 1:13)

7. John said that the one who came after him would baptize people with the Holy Spirit and _____. (Matthew 3:11)

10. John criticized Herod's marriage to _____. (Matthew 14:3-4)

11. The head of John was brought in on a _____. (Matthew 14:8)

12. John the Baptist ate this. (Matthew 3:4)

14. River where John baptized people. (Matthew 3:6)

18. John said someone would come after him whose _____ he would not be worthy to untie. (John 1:27)

WHO SAID IT?: MATCHING

Match the following people with the statement they made. Quotes are from the New King James Version of the Bible.

ADAM (Genesis 3:12)
ANGELS (Luke 2:14)
CROWD (Luke 23:18)
DELILAH (Judges 16:6)
GOD (Genesis 1:3)
JOB (Job 1:21)
JOHN THE BAPTIST (Matthew 3:3)
MARY (Luke 1:38)
MORDECAI (Esther 4:14)
NAOMI (Ruth 1:20)
PILATE (Matthew 27:24)
SHADRACH (Daniel 3:17–18)
SOLOMON (Song of Songs 2:10)
WOMAN AT THE WELL (John 4:17)

Quotes

1. _____ "Please tell me where your great strength lies, and with what you may be bound to afflict you."

2. _____ "I have no husband."

3. _____ "I am innocent of the blood of this just Person."

4. _____ "Let there be light."

5. _____ "The woman whom You gave to be with me, she gave me of the tree, and I ate."

6. _____ "Yet who knows whether you have come to the kingdom for such a time as this?"

7. _____ "If that is the case, our God whom we serve is able to deliver us from the burning fiery furnace, and He will deliver us from your hand, O king. But if not, let it be known to you, O king, that we do not serve your gods, nor will we worship the gold image which you have set up."

8. _____ "Call me Mara."

9. _____ "Release to us Barabbas."

10. _____ "The LORD gave, and the LORD has taken away; Blessed be the name of the LORD."

11. _____ "Prepare the way of the LORD."

12. _____ "Glory to God in the highest, and on earth peace, goodwill toward men!"

13. _____ "Behold the maidservant of the Lord! Let it be to me according to your word."

14. _____ "Rise up, my love, my fair one, and come away."

Answer key on page 134.

FALSE GODS AND IDOLS: WORD SEARCH

*Words may be horizontal, vertical, or diagonal,
forward or backward, and may overlap.*

```
U  U  K  K  O  T  H  B  E  N  O  T  H  O  A  U
T  D  N  B  V  S  N  F  C  B  J  X  Z  S  N  A
A  N  A  M  M  E  L  E  K  V  T  U  H  L  I  R
M  Q  C  J  A  D  A  P  R  K  B  E  L  A  B  T
M  H  Q  A  A  F  Z  M  E  G  R  V  N  A  H  E
U  V  T  G  S  P  L  L  O  A  A  I  O  B  A  M
Z  B  O  E  H  T  E  A  H  N  S  L  K  V  Z  I
R  N  G  D  R  M  O  X  C  R  W  E  X  L  N  S
N  E  B  O  M  O  O  R  O  N  L  T  U  C  O  K
T  Y  P  A  L  Q  T  K  S  O  E  B  A  H  M  U
V  J  R  A  Y  O  U  H  M  U  E  D  S  E  M  D
G  D  X  U  L  L  O  P  S  Z  E  N  L  M  I  R
A  K  A  T  R  A  T  W  L  A  Y  Z  J  O  R  A
C  H  D  S  E  M  R  E  H  M  E  K  D  S  G  M
F  A  U  Q  Z  F  E  A  M  I  H  S  A  H  N  V
T  G  J  F  B  B  G  J  L  W  D  I  F  E  D  T
```

ADRAMMELEK	BEL	NERGAL
AMON	CASTOR	NIBHAZ
ANAMMELEK	CHEMOSH	NISROK
ARTEMIS	DAGON	POLLUX
ASHERAH	GOLDEN CALF	RIMMON
ASHIMA	HERMES	TAMMUZ
ASHTORETH	MARDUK	TARTAK
BAAL	MOLEK	ZEUS
BEELZEBUL	NEBO	

BIBLICAL JUDGES AND THEIR ALLIES: WORD SEARCH

*Words may be horizontal, vertical, or diagonal,
forward or backward, and may overlap.*

```
G Z R U T K L H R O U B E A G R
I A H O U E S Y A C W G N O H E
B U L W I R H D E R E L O N C Y
Z A L N W G A W K U O Z J F J I
A I H F A O M O S S W B D A L F
N T R B A S G F R D S J E E K Y
O H D E U E A V N U S L B D S A
I O A J Z S R K Y H S A M S O N
N U G H O O W I V E I Z M J A U
Z H K I T M D R I A J Y S U A J
V Y M C D H Y K J Z I L I E E T
K A R A B E P C E M Z K X Y G L
J E P C F V O E Y R I L L M Z Z
A N B W O Q J N J K C P C G V D
```

ABDON
BARAK
DEBORAH
EHUD
ELI
ELON

GIDEON
IBZAN
JAEL
JAIR
JEPHTHAH
MOSES

OTHNIEL
SAMSON
SAMUEL
SHAMGAR
TOLA

*"The LORD raised up judges who delivered them out of the
hand of those who plundered them." —Judges 2:16 NKJV*

WEAPONS AND WIELDERS: MATCHING

*Each of these weapons was used by
a man or woman in the Bible. Match
the weapon with the wielder.*

A. DAVID
B. EHUD
C. GIDEON
D. JAEL
E. JESUS

F. JONATHAN
G. SAMSON
H. SAUL
I. SHAMGAR
J. WOMAN OF THEBEZ

_____ 1. Donkey's jawbone (Judges 15:15)

_____ 2. Double-edged shortsword (Judges 3:16)

_____ 3. Bow and arrow (2 Samuel 1:22)

_____ 4. Trumpet, jar, and torch (Judges 7:16–25)

_____ 5. Whip made of cords (John 2:15)

_____ 6. Oxgoad (Judges 3:31)

_____ 7. Millstone (Judges 9:53)

_____ 8. Tent peg (Judges 4:21)

_____ 9. Sling (1 Samuel 17:50)

_____ 10. Spear (1 Samuel 18:10–11)

*"They shall beat their swords into plowshares,
and their spears into pruning hooks; nation shall
not lift up sword against nation, neither shall
they learn war anymore." —Isaiah 2:4 NJKV*

GOD'S CREATION IN PSALM 148: WORD SEARCH

Words may be horizontal, vertical, or diagonal, forward or backward, and may overlap.

```
B  B  U  L  B  C  E  N  S  P  Q  S  S  M  D  L
R  I  G  L  E  T  A  T  R  P  O  N  V  Y  L  I
V  I  R  D  Q  E  A  F  O  U  E  O  B  S  Z  G
A  D  A  D  C  R  H  L  J  V  L  W  L  O  G  H
F  R  Z  O  S  V  B  A  C  K  E  J  N  M  T
S  N  U  S  A  L  J  E  S  M  G  I  R  E  A  N
H  N  P  I  H  I  H  B  U  N  F  I  N  S  G  I
O  S  I  S  F  A  P  O  A  A  U  B  D  G  Q  N
Q  N  C  A  D  H  A  N  I  M  A  L  S  M  S  G
T  O  U  P  T  U  S  A  F  S  A  C  N  O  O  M
H  I  L  L  S  N  O  E  H  C  C  A  O  S  D  Y
Y  T  L  J  S  C  U  L  E  Y  R  T  A  R  P  R
E  A  V  D  E  S  H  O  C  R  Y  T  B  E  W  K
M  N  N  W  O  M  E  N  M  E  T  L  A  T  V  J
N  I  P  P  S  O  P  R  I  N  C  E  S  A  G  S
W  J  U  N  E  R  D  L  I  H  C  B  V  W  O  D
```

ANGELS	HAIL	MOUNTAINS	SUN
ANIMALS	HEAVENS	NATIONS	TREES
BIRDS	HILLS	OCEAN	WATERS
CATTLE	KINGS	PRINCES	WINDS
CEDARS	LIGHTNING	RULERS	WOMEN
CHILDREN	MEN	SNOW	
CLOUDS	MOON	STARS	

BOOK OF HABAKKUK:
WHAT GOES TOGETHER?

*Read the prophet's words in the short,
three-chapter book of Habakkuk.*

*Using the following categories, create four
groups of four terms that belong together.*

Names for God

_____

_____

_____

_____

Attributes of God

_____

_____

_____

_____

**Metaphors for
Babylon**

_____

_____

_____

_____

**Attributes of the
Unrighteous**

_____

_____

_____

_____

My Holy One	Glory	Never at Rest	My Rock
Leopards	Mercy	Desert Wind	Puffed Up
My Savior	Arrogant	Eagle	Splendor
Wolves	Sovereign Lord	Power	Greedy

LESSER KNOWN 3:16s—
OLD TESTAMENT: MATCHING

*While John 3:16 is the most well known,
there are many other Bible verses that
can be found in chapter 3, verse 16. Match
the verse with the book of the Bible.*

A. GENESIS   E. 2 CHRONICLES   I. DANIEL
B. LEVITICUS   F. PROVERBS   J. NAHUM
C. NUMBERS   G. ECCLESIASTES
D. JUDGES   H. LAMENTATIONS

_____ 1. "So Moses counted them, as he was commanded by the word of the LORD."

_____ 2. "He made interwoven chains and put them on top of the pillars. He also made a hundred pomegranates and attached them to the chains."

_____ 3. "And I saw something else under the sun: In the place of judgment—wickedness was there, in the place of justice—wickedness was there."

_____ 4. "Long life is in her right hand; in her left hand are riches and honor."

_____ 5. "Now Ehud had made a double-edged sword about a cubit long, which he strapped to his right thigh under his clothing."

_____ 6. "He has broken my teeth with gravel; he has trampled me in the dust."

_____ 7. "Shadrach, Meshach and Abednego replied to him, 'King Nebuchadnezzar, we do not need to defend ourselves before you in this matter.'"

_____ 8. "You have increased the number of your merchants till they are more numerous than the stars in the sky, but like locusts they strip the land and then fly away."

_____ 9. "The priest shall burn them on the altar as a food offering, a pleasing aroma. All the fat is the LORD's."

_____ 10. "I will make your pains in childbearing very severe; with painful labor you will give birth to children. Your desire will be for your husband, and he will rule over you."

—— Answer key on page 136. ——

THE STORY OF SAMSON: WORD SEARCH

Words may be horizontal, vertical, or diagonal, forward or backward, and may overlap.

```
D E T P M G B P Q E U E H G P S
J N H I A I I Y F Y L C T J H G
O O I Z R L L V D P E Z G N I A
O B A L L I H L M R Y U N R L T
P W A A B A P E S S Q E E I I E
R A R I L Q T S T T R R R K S Y
Y J F I P F T L C V O N T Y T Q
O E L O Z N B O Q N S N S U I W
E E N E X T U C R I A H E M N R
D V F O L I O N U C K O R N E R
H L Z U H E U P F F H T W O V A
S H K H G P D O N K E Y W G B A
E L D D I R T I M N A H E A L R
C Z U K H Z W H K T I J E D S J
X J N G K F X B U K I P D Z C K
L A Y A R T E B K H R K I C T B
```

BETRAYAL	GATE	LION	STRENGTH
BLIND	GAZA	MILLSTONE	TEMPLE
DAGON	HAIRCUT	PHILISTINE	TIMNAH
DELILAH	HONEY	PILLAR	TORCH
DONKEY	JAWBONE	RIDDLE	
FOX	JUDGE	SPIRIT	

You can read the story of Samson in Judges 13–16.

HAIR AND BEARDS IN THE BIBLE: MULTIPLE CHOICE

Choose the correct answer.

1. In the Old Testament, men were required to shave their hair and beards to show they had recovered from this disease. (Leviticus 14:9)

   a. Fever

   b. Leprosy

   c. Dysentery

   d. Consumption

2. Absalom, the son of David, cut his hair at the end of every year when it became too heavy. At the end of the year, his hair weighed two hundred _____, which is about five pounds. (2 Samuel 14:26)

   a. Spans

   b. Talents

   c. Cubits

   d. Shekels

3. This man had red hair all over his body. (Genesis 25:25)

   a. Esau

   b. Jacob

   c. Samson

   d. John the Baptist

4. This man shaved himself with a sword to symbolize what would happen to Jerusalem. (Ezekiel 5:1–4)

   a. Ezra

   b. Jehoiakim

   c. Jaazaniah

   d. Ezekiel

5. As punishment for his pride, this man lived like a wild animal for seven years; his hair "grew like the feathers of an eagle." (Daniel 4:33)

   a. Pharaoh

   b. King Nebuchadnezzar

   c. Herod

   d. King Ahab

6. This man lost all his strength when his seven braids were cut. (Judges 16:19)

   a. Absalom

   b. Samson

   c. Esau

   d. Ehud

7. While fleeing from David's army, Absalom's hair got caught in _____, leaving him trapped and helpless. (2 Samuel 18:9)

a. An oak tree

b. The spokes of a chariot wheel

c. A door

d. A thornbush

8. Jacob disguised himself as his hairy brother Esau by covering his hands and neck with this. (Genesis 27:16)

a. Camel's hair

b. Sheep's wool

c. Goat skins

d. Bear fur

9. In order to escape harm from the King of Gath, David pretended to be insane by doing this. (1 Samuel 21:13)

a. Letting his hair grow wild and shaggy

b. Letting saliva run down his beard

c. Pulling out his beard by the roots

d. Burning his eyebrows

10. In John's vision in Revelation, Christ's hair was _____. (Revelation 1:14)

a. "Black like sackcloth, as black as night"

b. "White like wool, as white as snow"

c. "Yellow like gold, as yellow as the sun"

d. "Red like fire, as red as blood"

"But the very hairs of your head are all numbered. Do not fear therefore; you are of more value than many sparrows." —Luke 12:7 NKJV

Answer key on page 137.

SHEPHERDS AND SHEPHERDESSES: WORD SEARCH

Words may be horizontal, vertical, or diagonal, forward or backward, and may overlap.

```
R E H T M U I J N M U R D J N B
L J P L W S A L I Y B S E O O Y
C E E B S K B O M L J O E H E K
Z Z S L D O E T A W E M C H S G
T I O T E V L B J Y I V J A G A
V P J R E H R C N S H Z I U J N
G P B U N A C Z E D A H V N K E
S O M A H I S A B D A V I D T B
J R R A S R M B R D Y O M T T U
R A M A F B H S U G U P D G A E
Z H A V Y D D J W A A P C J J R
C C Z E B U L U N D M U E E H N
R A H C A S S I O O A L C V E U
I L A T H P A N S Y W O W P N Z
L A B A N V O E L K P I A A S V
R P O K M E S K T S N T D C J I
```

ABEL   DAVID   JOSEPH   NAPHTALI
ABRAHAM   DOEG   JUDAH   RACHEL
AMOS   GAD   LABAN   REUBEN
ASHER   ISAAC   LEVI   SIMEON
BENJAMIN   ISSACHAR   LOT   ZEBULUN
DAN   JACOB   MOSES   ZIPPORAH

*"I am the good shepherd. I know my own and
my own know me." —John 10:14 ESV*

Answer key on page 138.

LESSER KNOWN 3:16s—NEW TESTAMENT: MATCHING

While John 3:16 is the most well known, there are many other Bible verses that can be found in chapter 3, verse 16. Match the verse with the book of the Bible.

A. MATTHEW
B. LUKE
C. ROMANS

D. 1 CORINTHIANS
E. COLOSSIANS
F. 2 TIMOTHY

G. HEBREWS
H. 1 JOHN
I. REVELATION

_____ 1. "So, because you are lukewarm—neither hot nor cold—I am about to spit you out of my mouth."

_____ 2. "All Scripture is God-breathed and is useful for teaching, rebuking, correcting and training in righteousness."

_____ 3. "John answered them all, 'I baptize you with water. But one who is more powerful than I will come, the straps of whose sandals I am not worthy to untie. He will baptize you with the Holy Spirit and fire.'"

_____ 4. "As soon as Jesus was baptized, he went up out of the water. At that moment heaven was opened, and he saw the Spirit of God descending like a dove and alighting on him."

_____ 5. "This is how we know what love is: Jesus Christ laid down his life for us. And we ought to lay down our lives for our brothers and sisters."

_____ 6. "Let the message of Christ dwell among you richly as you teach and admonish one another with all wisdom through psalms, hymns, and songs from the Spirit, singing to God with gratitude in your hearts."

_____ 7. "Don't you know that you yourselves are God's temple and that God's Spirit dwells in your midst?"

_____ 8. "Who were they who heard and rebelled? Were they not all those Moses led out of Egypt?"

_____ 9. "Ruin and misery mark their ways."

THE FRUIT OF THE SPIRIT IS . . .
SELF-CONTROL: WORD SEARCH

*Self-control is a fruit of the Spirit described
throughout the Bible. Quotations are
from the English Standard Version.*

Whoever is **SLOW** to anger has great **UNDERSTANDING**, but he who has a hasty temper exalts folly. (Proverbs 14:29)

FLEE from sexual immorality. (1 Corinthians 6:18)

God is **FAITHFUL**, and he will not let you be tempted beyond your ability, but with the temptation he will also provide the way of **ESCAPE**, that you may be able to **ENDURE** it. (1 Corinthians 10:13)

Through **LOVE SERVE** one another. (Galatians 5:13)

WALK by the **SPIRIT**, and you will not gratify the desires of the flesh. (Galatians 5:16)

Be **STRONG** in the **LORD** and in the **STRENGTH** of his **MIGHT**. (Ephesians 6:10)

Let every person be quick to **HEAR**, slow to speak, slow to anger. (James 1:19)

Find the bolded words in the puzzle.
Words may be horizontal, vertical, or diagonal,
forward or backward, and may overlap.

```
E F L E E K F C Z T B U O Z
S Q F D P L G O I K Z T S G
C J Q K M A M R S T R O N G
A T Q I V W I R A E H I S R
P F G O L P E V O L D H T W
E H A A S P W W Q N A Y R V
T W P I K M O M A J E J E I
Z P I F T H L T E N Q T N R
T G Q K M H S L D K Z A G Y
E Z D E G R F U O X T Y T V
C V H Z E P R U J R B Z H P
F F R D O E C T L U D R L D
C I N E J B F B R E E K D N
O U I W S G Q R P K J O P G
```

NAOMI AND RUTH: CROSSWORD

*The answers to this puzzle are all
found in the book of Ruth.*

Across

5. Boaz's great-grandson (4:22)
6. The place Boaz went to transact legal business (4:1)
9. Attribute of God, which Ruth and Boaz were commended for (3:10)
10. Grain being gathered when Naomi and Ruth arrived in Judah (1:22)
11. Ruth did this to separate the kernels from the chaff (2:17)
12. Ruth's son (4:17)
14. Ruth wasn't native to Judah but was a _____ (2:10)
16. Quantity of grain Ruth gathered in one day (2:17)
18. Boaz was a _____ of Naomi's husband (3:2)
19. Naomi told Ruth to put this on before going out at night (3:3)
21. Boaz spread this part of his garment over Ruth (3:9)

Down

1. Boaz poured six measures of grain into this (3:15)
2. Country Ruth was from (1:4)
3. Book of Ruth took place during the time of the _____ (1:1)
4. Mara (1:20)
7. Naomi's husband (1:2)
8. Boaz declared Ruth "a woman of _____ character" (3:11)
12. Ruth's sister-in-law (1:4)
13. Naomi's hometown, to which she and Ruth relocated (1:19)
15. Ruth worked until this grain was gathered (2:23)
17. Witnesses to Boaz's purchase of Naomi's land (4:2)
20. Natural disaster Naomi fled (1:1)

TURN YOUR EYES UPON JESUS:
WORD SEARCH

Helen Howarth Lemmel (1863–1961) wrote the hymn "Turn Your Eyes upon Jesus" after reading a pamphlet written by Lilias Trotter, a lifelong missionary to the people of Algeria. The lyrics reflect the truths of Hebrews 12:2; John 8:12 and 10:10; and Romans 8:37.

O soul, are you **WEARY** and **TROUBLED**?
No light in the **DARKNESS** you see?
There's **LIGHT** for a look at the **SAVIOR**,
and life more **ABUNDANT** and free!

Turn your eyes upon **JESUS**,
look full in His **WONDERFUL** face,
and the things of **EARTH** will grow **STRANGELY** dim,
in the light of His **GLORY** and **GRACE**.

Through **DEATH** into life **EVERLASTING**,
He passed, and we **FOLLOW** Him there;
o'er us sin no more hath **DOMINION**—
for more than **CONQUERORS** we are!

His **WORD** shall not fail you—He **PROMISED**;
BELIEVE Him, and all will be well:
then go to a **WORLD** that is dying,
His **PERFECT SALVATION** to tell!

Find the bolded words in the puzzle.
Words may be horizontal, vertical, or diagonal,
forward or backward, and may overlap.

```
S N S A V L A B E P E Y D O N E
R O S B L A N B E L W R W I L V
O I E M E J Y R U O S O O J P E
R T N U T L F L N N I L R U M R
E A K L N E I D E M D G L U C L
U V R A C F E E E G L A D O J A
Q L A T O R T S V L N E N Y E S
N A D L F H I Q U E B A O T S T
O S L U G S A V I O R U R E U I
C O L I D E A T H T S E O T S N
W I L Q U D J E S Y C T U R S G
U Y R A E W H T R A E M P J T U
N O I N I M O D R Q U D S A C I
G U E W J D O G A T R A E L G D
P R O M I S E D R O C A M Y C H
O W N J U M L E W L E A Q U A F
```

THE FRUIT OF THE SPIRIT IS . . .
PATIENCE: CROSSWORD

Across

4. "But the _____ of the Spirit is love, joy, peace, forbearance, kindness, goodness, faithfulness." (Galatians 5:22)

7. "Better a patient person than a warrior, one with _____-_____ than one who takes a city." (Proverbs 16:32)

8. "Imitate those who through _____ and patience inherit what has been promised." (Hebrews 6:12)

11. "If we are comforted, it is for your comfort, which produces in you patient _____ of the same sufferings we suffer." (2 Corinthians 1:6)

13. "Be joyful in hope, patient in affliction, faithful in _____." (Romans 12:12)

15. "Be completely humble and gentle; be patient, _____ with one another in love." (Ephesians 4:2)

16. "Be _____ before the LORD and wait patiently for him." (Psalm 37:7)

Down

1. "You too, be patient and stand _____, because the Lord's coming is near." (James 5:8)

2. "A person's _____ yields patience; it is to one's glory to overlook an offense." (Proverbs 19:11)

3. "Through patience a ruler can be persuaded, and a _____ tongue can break a bone." (Proverbs 25:15)

5. "I was shown _____ so that in me, the worst of sinners, Christ Jesus might display his immense patience . . ." (1 Timothy 1:16)

6. "The Lord . . . is patient with you, not wanting anyone to perish, but everyone to come to _____." (2 Peter 3:9)

9. "After waiting patiently, Abraham received what was _____." (Hebrews 6:15)

10. "If we _____ for what we do not yet have, we wait for it patiently." (Romans 8:25)

12. "A hot-tempered person stirs up conflict, but the one who is patient _____ a quarrel." (Proverbs 15:18)

14. "Be patient, then, brothers and sisters, until the Lord's coming. See how the farmer _____ for the land to yield its valuable crop, patiently waiting for the autumn and spring rains." (James 5:7)

RULERS AND THEIR KINGDOMS: MATCHING

Match each ruler with the land they ruled.

___ 1.	Amraphel (Genesis 14:1)	a.	Roman Empire
___ 2.	Melchizedek (Genesis 14:18)	b.	Moab
___ 3.	Abimelek (Genesis 20:1–2)	c.	Palestine
___ 4.	Bela (Genesis 36:32)	d.	Egypt
___ 5.	Sihon (Numbers 21:26)	e.	Israel
___ 6.	Og (Numbers 21:33)	f.	Ethiopia
___ 7.	Balak (Numbers 22:4)	g.	Tyre
___ 8.	Achish (1 Samuel 21:10)	h.	Assyria
___ 9.	Hanun (2 Samuel 10:1)	i.	Shinar
___ 10.	Hiram (1 Kings 5:1)	j.	Babylon
___ 11.	Shishak (1 Kings 11:40)	k.	Gerar
___ 12.	Rehoboam (1 Kings 12:17)	l.	Salem
___ 13.	Ahab (1 Kings 16:29)	m.	Bashan
___ 14.	Hazael (1 Kings 19:15)	n.	Edom
___ 15.	Tiglath-pileser (2 Kings 15:29)	o.	Judah
___ 16.	Nebuchadnezzar (2 Kings 25:1)	p.	Ammon
___ 17.	Xerxes (Esther 1:1–3)	q.	Gath
___ 18.	Herod the Great (Matthew 2:1–3)	r.	Persia
___ 19.	Caesar Augustus (Luke 2:1)	s.	Aram
___ 20.	Kandake (Acts 8:27)	t.	Heshbon

"May all kings bow down to him and all nations serve him."
—Psalm 72:11

Answer key on page 142.

DEVOTED MOTHERS AND GRANDMOTHERS:
WORD SEARCH

*Words may be horizontal, vertical, or diagonal,
forward or backward, and may overlap.*

```
A R U S C Z E R K S J O B E H Z
R B E T H A N O W A I J O A R I
H L E B O S I O S Y L O I N M P
H A R H E G A M I H T U L Z I P
T U G O S K I D N T R A G M S O
A S N A C H A N N E M Z O D A R
H S E M R U T H Z B O A Z E R A
P H A T H S I A D A N R U C E H
E V E H A E L A B Z A B E C J Y
R E C R U I A H R I V D I O S R
A R A M A T G A U L O N C A F A
Z H R U T J O N T E U H I W T M
H T A N E S A N H E E N A O M W
Z E R U H O T A I B T N I C E N
R A C H E L J H E A R A G A Z O
L E A T H S H D R U N Z A N I L
```

ASENATH

BATHSHEBA

ELIZABETH

EUNICE

EVE

HAGAR

HANNAH

JOCHEBED

LEAH

LOIS

MARY

NAOMI

RACHEL

REBEKAH

RUTH

SARAH

TAMAR

(WIDOW OF) NAIN

(WIDOW OF) ZAREPHATH

ZERUIAH

ZIPPORAH

THE BEATITUDES: WORD SEARCH

Matthew 5:1–12 NKJV

And seeing the **MULTITUDES**, He went up on a **MOUNTAIN**, and when He was seated His **DISCIPLES** came to Him. Then He opened His mouth and **TAUGHT** them, saying:

"**BLESSED** are the **POOR** in **SPIRIT**,
　For theirs is the **KINGDOM** of heaven.
Blessed are those who **MOURN**,
　For they shall be **COMFORTED**.
Blessed are the **MEEK**,
　For they shall **INHERIT** the **EARTH**.
Blessed are those who hunger and thirst for
　RIGHTEOUSNESS,
　For they shall be **FILLED**.
Blessed are the **MERCIFUL**,
　For they shall obtain mercy.
Blessed are the **PURE** in **HEART**,
　For they shall see God.
Blessed are the **PEACEMAKERS**,
　For they shall be called sons of **GOD**.
Blessed are those who are **PERSECUTED** for
　righteousness' sake,
　For theirs is the kingdom of **HEAVEN**.

　Blessed are you when they revile and persecute you, and say all kinds of evil against you falsely for My sake. **REJOICE** and be exceedingly glad, for great is your **REWARD** in heaven, for so they persecuted the **PROPHETS** who were before you."

Find the bolded words in the puzzle.
Words may be horizontal, vertical, or diagonal,
forward or backward, and may overlap.

```
A P E C I O J E R I D H T R A E
M E R O U S L U F I C R E M O U
E A R M I B L E S S P I R E S T
E C E F N I L C O N F R O U S N
N E V O P I I E G O T A I D E R
K M I R P P A B S H E A V E N U
R A W T L R D T A S H E M T S O
C K L E F D O R N V E N P U U M
D E S D T H E P A U G D K C O W
O R I P S A P L H W O B I E E R
G S L N R I U B L E E M N S T O
K I N O H T R G L I T R G R H N
E M O C R E E L H U F S D E G U
E P L A V D R A S T L A O P I C
B R E S P I R I T H A F M O R A
F H I M U L T I T U D E S G H T
```

SPECIAL DAYS AND CELEBRATIONS:
WORD SEARCH

Words may be horizontal, vertical, or diagonal, forward or backward, and may overlap.

```
C O D A Y P R E N H U T S T U G
A H N D B D A L T I S P E O D A
G O R I N S P O N O B B L U F R
D O L I T E K K C E S A C V P E
S A O E S K V E R T U D A A H V
I T R D U T T A E B E R N H S O
N O D S F N M P E M I P R S U S
U N S D E R M A A L O W E E K S
S E D P R U I U S H U A B B T A
Y M A L R T N D Y O T U A M R P
D E Y T O D Y M A B B A T H U R
U N C O Y S T E P Y R I B E E K
H T S T I U R F T S R I F B U R
Y A D N U S M L A P U R I M A S
Y O M H A N A H S A H H S O R S
F I R F U Y O M K I P P U R M Y
```

CHRISTMAS
(DAY OF) ATONEMENT
EASTER
(FEAST OF) FIRSTFRUITS
(FEAST OF) TABERNACLES
(FEAST OF) TRUMPETS
(FEAST OF) WEEKS
GOOD FRIDAY
LORD'S DAY
MAUNDY (THURSDAY)

PALM SUNDAY
PASSOVER
PENTECOST
PURIM
ROSH HASHANAH
SABBATH
SHAVUOT
SUKKOTH
YOM KIPPUR

"This is a day you are to commemorate." —Exodus 12:14

THE FRUIT OF THE SPIRIT: TEST YOUR MEMORY

Throughout this book, you've worked one puzzle page for each fruit of the Holy Spirit. Test your knowledge and see how many of these fruit you can list from memory. Check your answers with Galatians 5:22–23.

_____

_____

_____

_____

_____

_____

_____

_____

THE SHEMA: WORD SEARCH

Deuteronomy 6:4–9 ESV

Hear, O **ISRAEL**: The LORD our God, the LORD is one. You shall **LOVE** the **LORD** your God with all your **HEART** and with all your **SOUL** and with all your **MIGHT**. And these **WORDS** that I **COMMAND** you today shall be on your heart. You shall **TEACH** them **DILIGENTLY** to your **CHILDREN**, and shall talk of them when you sit in your **HOUSE**, and when you **WALK** by the way, and when you lie down, and when you **RISE**. You shall **BIND** them as a **SIGN** on your **HAND**, and they shall be as **FRONTLETS** between your **EYES**. You shall **WRITE** them on the **DOORPOSTS** of your house and on your **GATES**.

When asked what the greatest commandment in God's law is, Jesus quoted this Old Testament passage known to Jesus and His hearers as the Shema (pronounced shuh-MAH).

Find the bolded words in the puzzle.
Words may be horizontal, vertical, or diagonal,
forward or backward, and may overlap.

```
I   S   A   R   E   N   T   S   O   L   L   T   H   A
F   R   O   T   L   H   E   M   O   N   U   E   A   H
E   V   O   L   G   E   V   R   I   S   O   A   N   I
M   I   G   I   F   A   D   H   E   S   S   C   D   D
O   N   M   T   S   E   Y   E   T   T   F   H   I   U
E   T   A   G   R   Y   E   S   O   R   I   L   O   V
B   I   N   D   I   A   O   C   O   M   I   R   L   A
G   A   T   E   S   P   E   N   O   G   S   E   W   N
O   R   D   L   R   O   T   H   E   M   C   I   E   D
E   Y   S   O   A   L   S   N   E   A   M   S   G   O
K   S   O   H   E   A   T   H   G   M   I   A   W   N
L   D   U   T   L   L   A   W   O   R   D   S   N   U
A   L   S   O   Y   N   E   R   D   L   I   H   C   D
W   O   R   L   H   E   A   D   N   I   P   A   T   C
```

BIRTH OF JESUS: WHAT GOES TOGETHER?

*Read about Jesus's birth in Matthew
1:18–2:23 and Luke 1:1–2:40.*

*Using the following categories, create four
groups of four terms that belong together.*

**Divine Messengers
& Messages**

_____

_____

_____

_____

**Witnesses to
the Messiah**

_____

_____

_____

_____

Unlikely Mothers

_____

_____

_____

_____

People in Power

_____

_____

_____

_____

Wise Men	Old Age	Anna	Herod
Dreams	Simeon	Quirinius	Mary
Caesar Augustus	Elizabeth	Gabriel	Shepherds
Heavenly Host	Archelaus	Virgin	Angel of the Lord

GIFTS OF THE SPIRIT: WORD SEARCH

Romans 12:4-8

Just as each of us has one **BODY** with many members, and these **MEMBERS** do not all have the same **FUNCTION**, so in **CHRIST** we, though many, form one body, and each member **BELONGS** to all the others. We have **DIFFERENT** gifts, according to the **GRACE** given to each of us. If your **GIFT** is prophesying, then **PROPHESY** in accordance with your **FAITH**; if it is **SERVING**, then serve; if it is **TEACHING**, then teach; if it is to **ENCOURAGE**, then give encouragement; if it is **GIVING**, then give **GENEROUSLY**; if it is to **LEAD**, do it **DILIGENTLY**; if it is to show **MERCY**, do it **CHEERFULLY**.

Find the bolded words in the puzzle.
Words may be horizontal, vertical, or diagonal,
forward or backward, and may overlap.

```
B  O  T  Y  T  E  A  H  N  C  O  Y  F  M
I  E  H  N  E  F  A  I  H  O  S  L  U  E
F  R  L  C  E  L  I  E  B  O  G  T  N  R
L  A  A  O  B  R  E  G  O  R  N  N  C  C
T  R  I  A  N  R  E  P  D  B  I  E  T  Y
G  O  N  T  F  G  R  F  Y  U  V  G  I  G
B  E  L  U  H  A  S  O  F  M  I  I  O  N
E  N  L  E  A  D  G  M  C  I  G  L  N  I
Y  L  S  U  O  R  E  N  E  G  D  I  M  H
Y  S  E  H  P  O  R  P  I  M  A  D  E  C
D  I  F  T  S  I  R  H  C  V  B  O  D  A
M  E  N  C  O  U  R  A  G  E  R  E  Y  E
G  N  I  H  C  D  I  L  I  M  E  E  R  T
L  O  N  S  G  Y  C  E  V  I  G  N  S  S
```

BLESSED ASSURANCE: WORD SEARCH

*Moved by music composed by her friend
Phoebe Palmer Knapp, Fanny Crosby
(1820–1915) wrote the words to "Blessed
Assurance." Crosby drew her lyrics from the
promises of 1 Peter 1:8 and 1 John 3:1–3.*

Blessed **ASSURANCE**, Jesus is mine!
Oh, what a **FORETASTE** of glory **DIVINE**!
Heir of salvation, **PURCHASE** of God,
born of his Spirit, **WASHED** in his **BLOOD**.

This is my **STORY**, this is my song,
PRAISING my Savior all the day long.
This is my story, this is my **SONG**,
praising my **SAVIOR** all the day long.

Perfect **COMMUNION**, perfect **DELIGHT**,
VISIONS of **RAPTURE** now burst on my sight.
ANGELS descending bring from above
ECHOES of mercy, **WHISPERS** of love.

PERFECT submission, all is at rest.
I in my Savior am happy and **BLESSED**,
WATCHING and **WAITING**, looking above,
filled with his **GOODNESS**, lost in his love.

Find the bolded words in the puzzle.
Words may be horizontal, vertical, or diagonal,
forward or backward, and may overlap.

```
W E G N A T C H R A E N O R W E
V A C O L E H I D E T O H A A B
G I S N S E O H C E S T E P I M
O N S H A P U R C H A S E T T O
O B O I E R S E A S T Y R U I S
H A Y S O D U N Y O E B O R N U
G R A C S N G S R N R L I E G P
E N B L R E S Y S T O O V M A N
M A T U L A I R E A F O A B O T
G N I S I A R P E R S D S I H C
O F F U L E G A T P E U N T U E
U S S E N D O O G S S U L R I F
D E L I G H T R S E M I P O E R
A R V I E B N E R M I S H U P E
W I G E F U L S O A B D O W I P
D I N R S B Y C W A T C H I N G
```

WORD SEARCH
& ACTIVITY BOOK

SOLUTIONS

AND

ANSWERS

BOOKS OF THE BIBLE: OLD TESTAMENT

13	1 Chronicles	18	Job
11	1 Kings	29	Joel
9	1 Samuel	32	Jonah
14	2 Chronicles	6	Joshua
12	2 Kings	7	Judges
10	2 Samuel	25	Lamentations
30	Amos	3	Leviticus
27	Daniel	39	Malachi
5	Deuteronomy	33	Micah
21	Ecclesiastes	34	Nahum
17	Esther	16	Nehemiah
2	Exodus	4	Numbers
26	Ezekiel	31	Obadiah
15	Ezra	20	Proverbs
1	Genesis	19	Psalms
35	Habakkuk	8	Ruth
37	Haggai	22	Song of Songs
28	Hosea	38	Zechariah
23	Isaiah	36	Zephaniah
24	Jeremiah		

BOOKS OF THE BIBLE: NEW TESTAMENT

7	1 Corinthians	9	Galatians
23	1 John	19	Hebrews
21	1 Peter	20	James
13	1 Thessalonians	4	John
15	1 Timothy	26	Jude
8	2 Corinthians	3	Luke
24	2 John	2	Mark
22	2 Peter	1	Matthew
14	2 Thessalonians	18	Philemon
16	2 Timothy	11	Philippians
25	3 John	27	Revelation
5	Acts	6	Romans
12	Colossians	17	Titus
10	Ephesians		

JONAH AND THE HUGE FISH: WORD SEARCH

THE FRUIT OF THE SPIRIT IS . . . LOVE:
FILL IN THE BLANK

1. angels, gong, knowledge, faith, poor, love
2. conflict, wrongs
3. sincere, good
4. truth, trusts
5. humble, patient
6. faith, hope, love

BIBLE VILLAINS: WORD SEARCH

```
J  U  R  U  H  F  B  H  X  P  L  A  M  P  G  B
U  W  J  Y  Q  Q  A  M  X  H  H  B  X  B  Z  Q
D  A  B  I  M  E  L  E  K  H  T  A  R  S  S  N
A  H  T  M  I  O  A  D  K  Y  E  A  R  E  M  V
S  I  D  H  F  F  A  H  E  R  O  D  I  A  S  T
F  T  I  G  A  J  M  M  T  D  Z  G  G  L  O  F
C  J  K  N  Y  L  Q  J  O  M  R  P  Z  R  O  H
N  K  N  A  V  H  I  R  O  L  F  C  L  C  P  G
A  E  I  M  D  L  E  A  Z  T  A  H  X  A  H  Y
Z  V  R  A  O  H  J  G  H  I  N  Y  V  W  A  T
D  O  C  H  Q  V  L  E  N  N  Z  Q  W  S  R  J
T  N  E  P  R  E  S  C  Z  K  R  A  U  S  I  E
N  E  B  U  C  H  A  D  N  E  Z  Z  A  R  S  E
H  A  L  I  L  E  D  H  T  Q  B  T  V  J  E  O
Y  F  I  D  W  Z  U  A  T  B  A  E  S  L  E  T
J  Q  S  E  K  E  G  N  Q  N  I  I  L  C  S  K
```

RUN, RUN, RUN: CROSSWORD

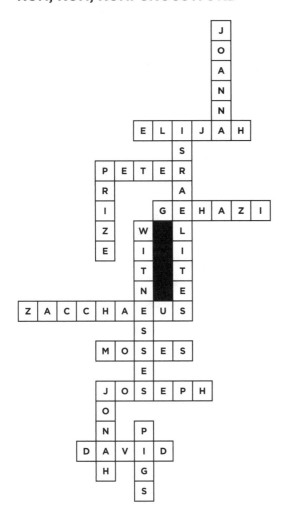

JOHN 3:16-17: WORD SEARCH

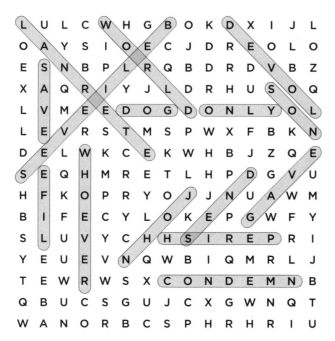

PSALM 23: FILL IN THE BLANK

1. shepherd
2. pastures
3. waters
4. righteousness
5. shadow
6. evil
7. comfort
8. enemies
9. cup
10. follow
11. Lord

ALL THINGS BRIGHT AND BEAUTIFUL: WORD SEARCH

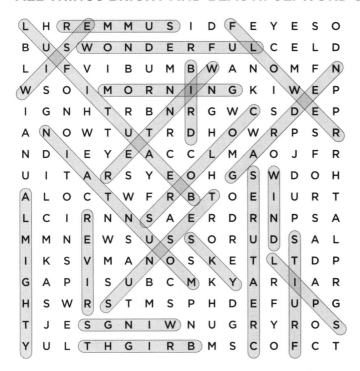

LANDS OF THE BIBLE TODAY: CROSSWORD

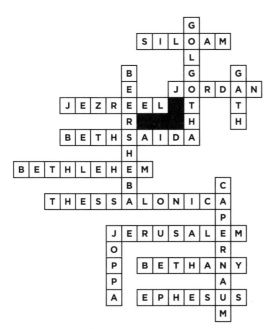

RAISING OF LAZARUS: WHAT GOES TOGETHER?

Family Members

Martha

Sisters

Mary

Lazarus

Words of Jesus

Lazarus, Come Out!

Take Away the Stone

I Am the Resurrection

You Will See the Glory of God

Titles of Jesus

Messiah

Rabbi

Teacher

Lord

Lazarus's Tomb

Cave

Stone

Odor

Strips of Linen

THE POWER OF WORDS: FILL IN THE BLANK

1. life, death
2. joy, timely
3. multiplying, prudent
4. waters, wisdom
5. fools, snare
6. grace, salt, everyone
7. trusted, kisses
8. prepared, hope, gentleness, respect

THE POWER OF WORDS: WORD SEARCH

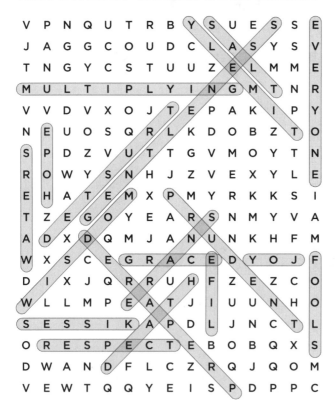

COMMON SAYINGS FROM THE OLD TESTAMENT: MATCHING

1. K	7. I
2. C	8. F
3. E	9. B
4. H	10. D
5. A	11. J
6. G	12. L

COMMON SAYINGS FROM THE NEW TESTAMENT: MATCHING

1. L	7. F
2. A	8. K
3. I	9. J
4. B	10. D
5. C	11. E
6. G	12. H

CHRISTMAS STORY: WORD SEARCH

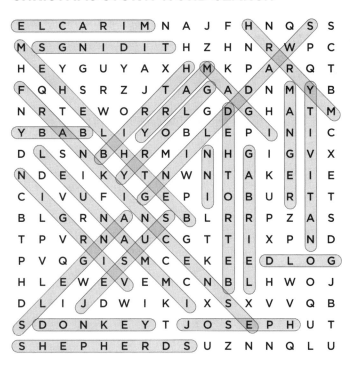

PEOPLE KNOWN BY TWO NAMES: WORD SCRAMBLE

1. Abraham
2. Abednego
3. Daniel
4. Shadrach
5. Jacob
6. Solomon
7. Meshach
8. Sarah
9. Paul
10. Peter

MORE LANDS OF THE BIBLE TODAY: CROSSWORD

MUSICAL INSTRUMENTS IN THE BIBLE: WORD SEARCH

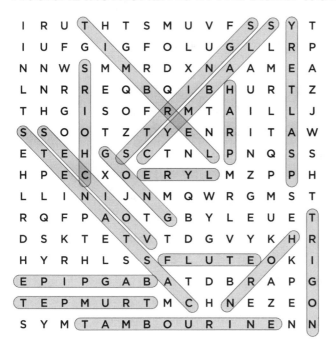

THE FRUIT OF THE SPIRIT IS . . . JOY: FILL IN THE BLANK

1. strength
2. joy, truth
3. commands, Father's, complete
4. praise, delivered

5. glorious, salvation
6. grief, rejoice
7. righteous, wicked

ISAIAH 40:28–31: FILL IN THE BLANK

1. know
2. heard
3. everlasting
4. Creator
5. earth
6. tired
7. weary
8. understanding
9. strength
10. power

11. tired
12. stumble
13. hope
14. renew
15. wings
16. eagles
17. run
18. walk
19. faint
20. Isaiah

ISAIAH 40:28-31: WORD SEARCH

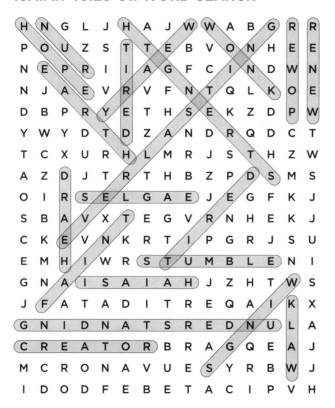

PRIESTLY GARMENTS: MINI CROSS

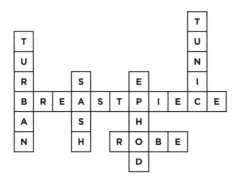

THE 7 I AMS OF JESUS: SCRIPTURE MATCH

1. John 6:35
2. John 10:9
3. John 10:11
4. John 8:12

5. John 11:25
6. John 15:1
7. John 14:6

HOLY, HOLY, HOLY: WORD SEARCH

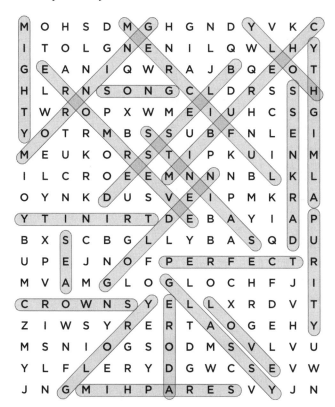

OLD TESTAMENT BIBLE SPOUSES: MATCHING

1. Boaz
2. Adam
3. Gomer
4. Abraham
5. Zipporah
6. Jacob
7. Hannah
8. King Xerxes
9. Leah
10. Samson
11. Isaac
12. Abigail

MYSTERY: DOUBLE PUZZLE

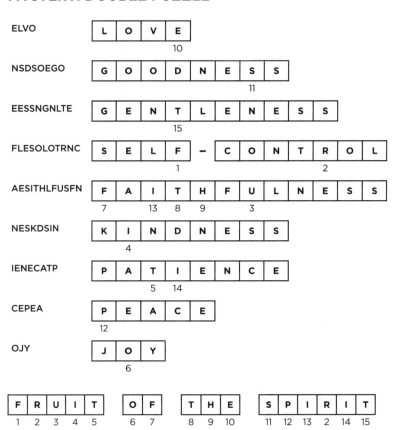

ELVO

L	O	V	E

10

NSDSOEGO

G	O	O	D	N	E	S	S

11

EESSNGNLTE

G	E	N	T	L	E	N	E	S	S

15

FLESOLOTRNC

S	E	L	F	–	C	O	N	T	R	O	L

1　　　　2

AESITHLFUSFN

F	A	I	T	H	F	U	L	N	E	S	S

7　　13　8　9　　3

NESKDSIN

K	I	N	D	N	E	S	S

4

IENECATP

P	A	T	I	E	N	C	E

5　14

CEPEA

P	E	A	C	E

12

OJY

J	O	Y

6

F	R	U	I	T
1	2	3	4	5

O	F
6	7

T	H	E
8	9	10

S	P	I	R	I	T
11	12	13	2	14	15

122

INSTRUCTION FOR PARENTS AND GRANDPARENTS:
WORD SEARCH

JOSEPH SOLD INTO SLAVERY: WHAT GOES TOGETHER?

Joseph's Brothers

Reuben
Judah
Simeon
Benjamin

Places

Canaan
Shechem
Valley of Hebron
Dothan

Dream Symbols

Sheaves of Grain
Sun
Moon
Eleven Stars

Merchant Goods

Camels
Spices
Myrrh
Balm

FISH TALES: CROSSWORD

THE FRUIT OF THE SPIRIT IS . . . PEACE:
MULTIPLE CHOICE

1. d
2. b
3. a

4. b
5. c

MAHERSHALALHASHBAZ: ARRANGE THE LETTERS

The longest word that can be made with this name is 9 letters: marshalls.

Other words you may have found: sharable, halalas, marsala, marbles, smaller, rashes, harems, alarm, balsa, smash, seal, earl, lamb, ash, ham, hah, ear.

Altogether there are **481 words of 3 letters or more** that can be made from this name!

BUT GOD . . . NEW TESTAMENT VERSES:
FILL IN THE BLANK

1. E
2. B
3. C

4. F
5. D
6. A

BOOKS OF THE BIBLE NAMED AFTER A PERSON— OLD TESTAMENT: WORD SEARCH

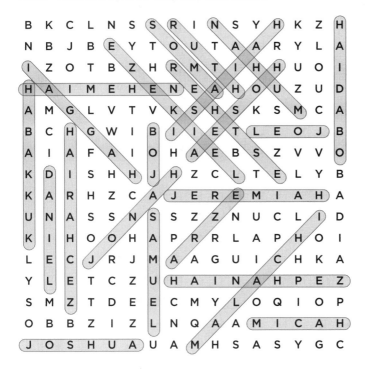

B K C L N S S R I N S Y H K Z H
N B J B E Y T O U T A A R Y L A
I Z O T B Z H R M T I H H U O I
H A I M E H E N E A H O U Z U D
A M G L V T V K S H S K S M C A
B C H G W I B I I E T L E O J B
A I A F A I O H A E B S Z V V O
K D I S H H J H Z C L T E L Y B
K A R H Z C A J E R E M I A H A
U N A S S N S S Z Z N U C L I D
K I H O O H A P R R L A P H O I
L E C J R J M A A G U I C H K A
Y L E T C Z U H A I N A H P E Z
S M Z T D E E C M Y L O Q I O P
O B B Z I Z L N Q A A M I C A H
J O S H U A U A M H S A S Y G C

GREAT IS THY FAITHFULNESS: WORD SEARCH

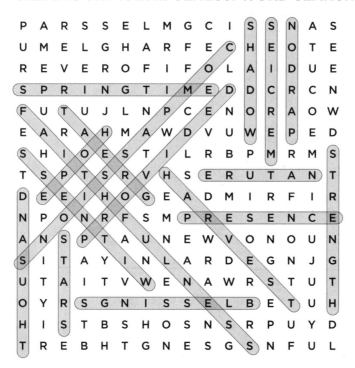

PARABLE OF THE PRODIGAL SON:
WHAT GOES TOGETHER?

The Father's Inheritance
Estate
Property
Share
Wealth

In a Distant Country
Wild Living
Famine
Pigs
Pods

The Father's Response
Compassion
Running
Hug
Kiss

Symbols of the Father's Favor
Robe
Ring
Sandals
Fattened Calf

MONEY: CROSSWORD

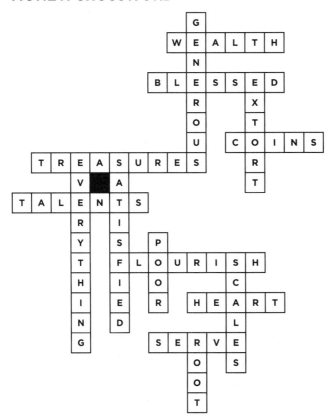

BOOKS OF THE NEW TESTAMENT: WORD SEARCH

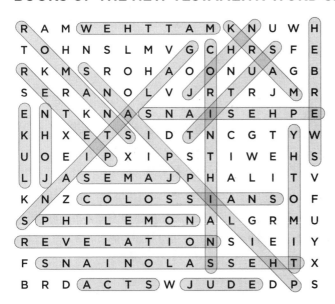

THE ARK OF THE COVENANT: MINI CROSS

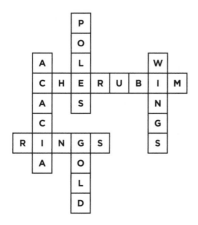

NUMBERS IN THE BIBLE: FILL IN THE BLANK

a. 30,000   e. 3,000   i. 500   m. 12,000   q. 7,000

b. 153   f. 5,000   j. 123   n. 175   r. 1,260

c. 969   g. 1,000   k. 150   o. 666

d. 120   h. 700   l. 144,000   p. 777

HEROES OF THE BIBLE: WORD SEARCH

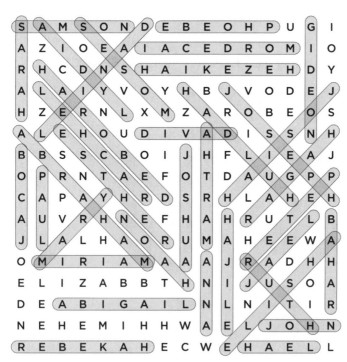

THE LIFE OF DAVID: WORD SEARCH

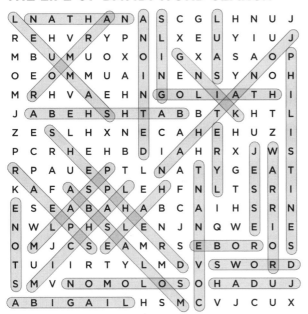

BIBLE PROFESSIONS: CROSSWORD

THE FRUIT OF THE SPIRIT IS . . . KINDNESS: WORD SCRAMBLE

1. Faithfulness
2. Favor
3. Forsaken
4. Withholds
5. Righteous
6. Everlasting
7. Compassion
8. Justice
9. Cords
10. Provides
11. Welcomed
12. Patience
13. Grace
14. Mercy

THE FRUIT OF THE SPIRIT IS . . . FAITHFULNESS: WORD SEARCH

THE FRUIT OF THE SPIRIT IS . . . GOODNESS: WORD SEARCH

THE FRUIT OF THE SPIRIT IS . . . GENTLENESS: WORD SCRAMBLE

1. Whisper
2. Mercy
3. Wrath
4. Patience
5. Humble
6. King
7. Spirit
8. Humility
9. Bearing
10. Evident
11. Kindness
12. Violent
13. Godliness
14. Peaceable
15. Quiet
16. Respect

THE LIFE & DEMISE OF JUDAS: CROSSWORD

SWING LOW, SWEET CHARIOT: WORD SEARCH

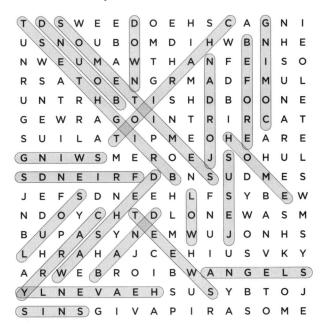

JOHN THE BAPTIST: CROSSWORD

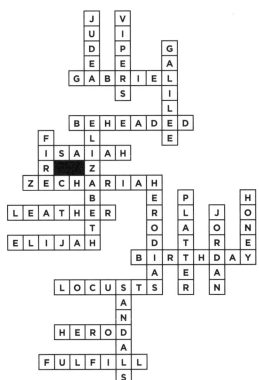

WHO SAID IT?: MATCHING

1. Delilah
2. Woman at the well
3. Pilate
4. God
5. Adam
6. Mordecai
7. Shadrach
8. Naomi
9. Crowd
10. Job
11. John the Baptist
12. Angels
13. Mary
14. Solomon

FALSE GODS AND IDOLS: WORD SEARCH

BIBLICAL JUDGES AND THEIR ALLIES: WORD SEARCH

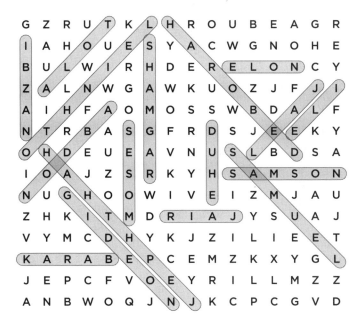

```
G  Z  R  U  T  K  L  H  R  O  U  B  E  A  G  R
I  A  H  O  U  E  S  Y  A  C  W  G  N  O  H  E
B  U  L  W  I  R  H  D  E  R  E  L  O  N  C  Y
Z  A  L  N  W  G  A  W  K  U  O  Z  J  F  J  I
A  I  H  F  A  O  M  O  S  S  W  B  D  A  L  F
N  T  R  B  A  S  G  F  R  D  S  J  E  E  K  Y
O  H  D  E  U  E  A  V  N  U  S  L  B  D  S  A
I  O  A  J  Z  S  R  K  Y  H  S  A  M  S  O  N
N  U  G  H  O  O  W  I  V  E  I  Z  M  J  A  U
Z  H  K  I  T  M  D  R  I  A  J  Y  S  U  A  J
V  Y  M  C  D  H  Y  K  J  Z  I  L  I  E  E  T
K  A  R  A  B  E  P  C  E  M  Z  K  X  Y  G  L
J  E  P  C  F  V  O  E  Y  R  I  L  L  M  Z  Z
A  N  B  W  O  Q  J  N  J  K  C  P  C  G  V  D
```

WEAPONS AND WIELDERS: MATCHING

1. G
2. B
3. F
4. C
5. E
6. I
7. J
8. D
9. A
10. H

GOD'S CREATION IN PSALM 148: WORD SEARCH

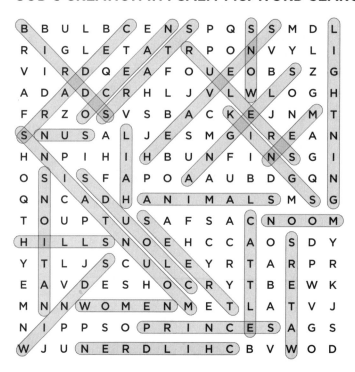

BOOK OF HABAKKUK: WHAT GOES TOGETHER?

Names for God

My Holy One
My Rock
My Savior
Sovereign Lord

Attributes of God

Mercy
Glory
Splendor
Power

Metaphors for Babylon

Leopards
Desert Wind
Eagle
Wolves

Attributes of the Unrighteous

Puffed Up
Arrogant
Never at Rest
Greedy

LESSER KNOWN 3:16s—OLD TESTAMENT: MATCHING

1. C
2. E
3. G
4. F
5. D

6. H
7. I
8. J
9. B
10. A

THE STORY OF SAMSON: WORD SEARCH

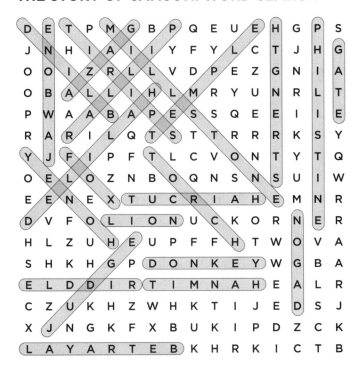

HAIR AND BEARDS IN THE BIBLE: MULTIPLE CHOICE

1. b
2. d
3. a
4. d
5. b
6. b
7. a
8. c
9. b
10. b

SHEPHERDS AND SHEPHERDESSES: WORD SEARCH

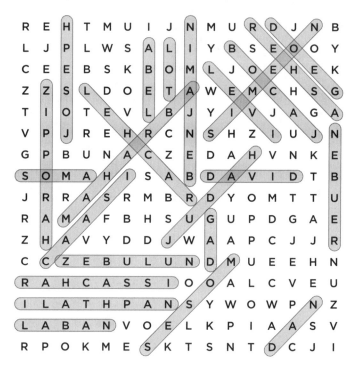

```
R  E  H  T  M  U  I  J  N  M  U  R  D  J  N  B
L  J  P  L  W  S  A  L  I  Y  B  S  E  O  O  Y
C  E  E  B  S  K  B  O  M  L  J  O  E  H  E  K
Z  Z  S  L  D  O  E  T  A  W  E  M  C  H  S  G
T  I  O  T  E  V  L  B  J  Y  I  V  J  A  G  A
V  P  J  R  E  H  R  C  N  S  H  Z  I  U  J  N
G  P  B  U  N  A  C  Z  E  D  A  H  V  N  K  E
S  O  M  A  H  I  S  A  B  D  A  V  I  D  T  B
J  R  R  A  S  R  M  B  R  D  Y  O  M  T  T  U
R  A  M  A  F  B  H  S  U  G  U  P  D  G  A  E
Z  H  A  V  Y  D  D  J  W  A  A  P  C  J  J  R
C  C  Z  E  B  U  L  U  N  D  M  U  E  E  H  N
R  A  H  C  A  S  S  I  O  O  A  L  C  V  E  U
I  L  A  T  H  P  A  N  S  Y  W  O  W  P  N  Z
L  A  B  A  N  V  O  E  L  K  P  I  A  A  S  V
R  P  O  K  M  E  S  K  T  S  N  T  D  C  J  I
```

LESSER KNOWN 3:16s—NEW TESTAMENT: MATCHING

1. I
2. F
3. B
4. A
5. H
6. E
7. D
8. G
9. C

THE FRUIT OF THE SPIRIT IS . . . SELF-CONTROL: WORD SEARCH

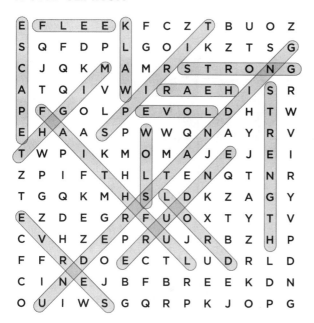

NAOMI AND RUTH: CROSSWORD

TURN YOUR EYES UPON JESUS: WORD SEARCH

THE FRUIT OF THE SPIRIT IS . . . PATIENCE: CROSSWORD

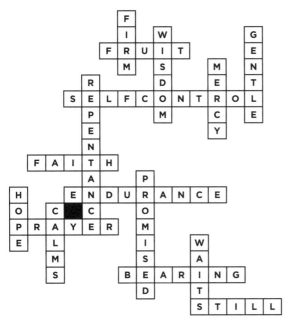

RULERS AND THEIR KINGDOMS: MATCHING

1. i	11. d
2. l	12. o
3. k	13. e
4. n	14. s
5. t	15. h
6. m	16. j
7. b	17. r
8. q	18. c
9. p	19. a
10. g	20. f

DEVOTED MOTHERS AND GRANDMOTHERS: WORD SEARCH

THE BEATITUDES: WORD SEARCH

```
A P E C I O J E R I D H T R A E
M E R O U S L U F I C R E M O U
E A R M I B L E S S P I R E S T
E C E F N I L C O N F R O U S N
N E V O P I I E G O T A I D E R
K M I R P P A B S H E A V E N U
R A W T L R D T A S H E M T S O
C K L E F D O R N V E N P U U M
D E S D T H E P A U G D K C O W
O R I P S A P L H W O B I E E R
G S L N R I U B L E E M N S T O
K I N O H T R G L I T R G R H N
E M O C R E E L H U F S D E G U
E P L A V D R A S T L A O P I C
B R E S P I R I T H A F M O R A
F H I M U L T I T U D E S G H T
```

SPECIAL DAYS AND CELEBRATIONS: WORD SEARCH

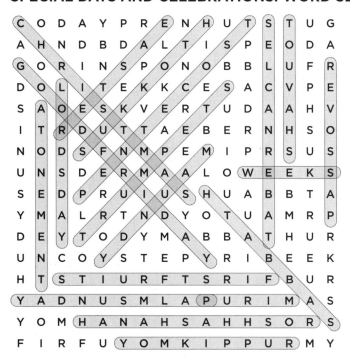

```
C O D A Y P R E N H U T S T U G
A H N D B D A L T I S P E O D A
G O R I N S P O N O B B L U F R
D O L I T E K K C E S A C V P E
S A O E S K V E R T U D A A H V
I T R D U T T A E B E R N H S O
N O D S F N M P E M I P R S U S
U N S D E R M A A L O W E E K S
S E D P R U I U S H U A B B T A
Y M A L R T N D Y O T U A M R P
D E Y T O D Y M A B B A T H U R
U N C O Y S T E P Y R I B E E K
H T S T I U R F T S R I F B U R
Y A D N U S M L A P U R I M A S
Y O M H A N A H S A H H S O R S
F I R F U Y O M K I P P U R M Y
```

THE FRUIT OF THE SPIRIT: TEST YOUR MEMORY

Love

Joy

Peace

Patience

Kindness

Goodness

Faithfulness

Gentleness

Self-Control

THE SHEMA: WORD SEARCH

BIRTH OF JESUS: WHAT GOES TOGETHER?

Divine Messengers & Messages

Gabriel

Angel of the Lord

Heavenly Host

Dreams

Unlikely Mothers

Elizabeth

Old Age

Mary

Virgin

Witnesses to the Messiah

Shepherds

Simeon

Anna

Wise Men

People in Power

Herod

Caesar Augustus

Quirinius

Archelaus

GIFTS OF THE SPIRIT: WORD SEARCH

BLESSED ASSURANCE: WORD SEARCH

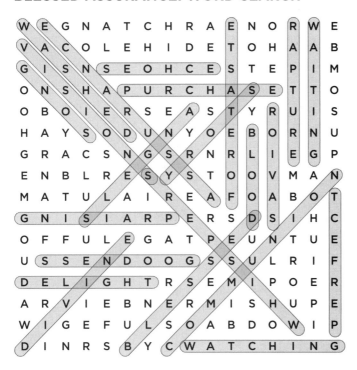

Spread the Word
by Doing One Thing.

- Give a copy of this book as a gift.
- Share the QR code link via your social media.
- Write a review of this book on your blog, favorite bookseller's website, or at ODB.org/store.
- Recommend this book to your church, small group, or book club.

Connect with us. 🅵 📷 🐦

Our Daily Bread Publishing
PO Box 3566, Grand Rapids, MI 49501, USA
Email: books@odb.org

Love God. Love Others.

with  Our Daily Bread.

Your gift changes lives.

Connect with us. [f] [◎] [𝕐]

Our Daily Bread Publishing
PO Box 3566, Grand Rapids, MI 49501, USA
Email: books@odb.org

Bible fun for anyone, anywhere, anytime

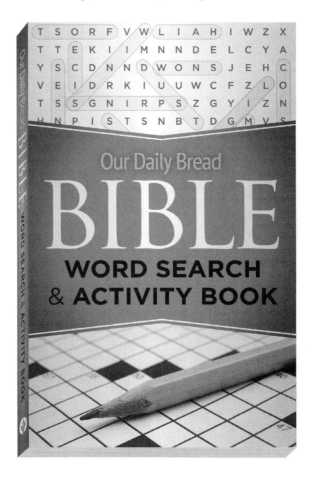

This Bible-based activity and fun book provides hours of entertainment with word searches, crosswords, and quizzes, all containing Scripture themes.

More Bible fun for game lovers!

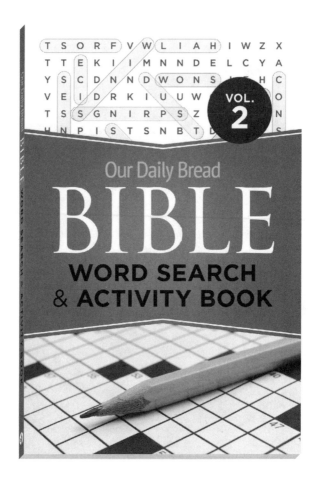

You'll find word searches, crossword puzzles, word scrambles, and so much more in this Bible-based activity book.

Jumbo fun for kids

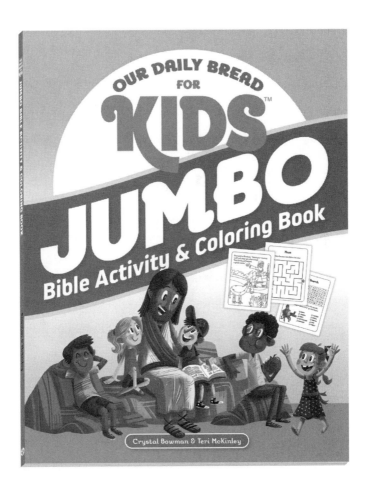

Children ages 6 to 9 will keep busy with this 200-page activity and coloring book compiled from the popular Our Daily Bread for Kids series. Occupy kids' curious minds, keep them focused on God's Word, and reduce their screen time!